D0480523

HEATH

All Gourmets Great And Small

All Gourmets Great And Small

By

Clive and Angela Russell-Taylor

Part of the proceeds of this book
will be donated to the R.S.P.C.A.

Ashford Press Publishing
Southampton
1988

Published by   Ashford Press Publishing 1988
1 Church Road
Shedfield
Hampshire SO3 2HW

© Clive and Angela Russell-Taylor, 1988

All rights reserved. Except for use in review, no part of this book may
be reproduced or utilised in any form or by any means electronic or
mechanical including photocopying, recording or by any information
storage and retrieval system, without permission from the publisher.

British Library Cataloguing in Publication Data

Russell-taylor, Clive
  All gourmets great and small.
  1. Pets 2. Food 3. Recipes
  I Title
  636.08'55

  ISBN 1-85253-048-0

Designed and typeset by Jordan and Jordan, Fareham, Hants

Printed and bound by Robert Hartnoll (1985) Ltd., Bodmin, Cornwall.

The authors and publishers wish to thank the following for
permission to use photographs: Howletts and Port Lympne Estates
Limited for "Djuom" the gorilla; Weidenfeld and Nicolson Ltd for Sir
John Mills and family.

"The Greatness Of A Nation And Its Moral Progress Can Be Judged By The Way Its Animals Are Treated."

(Ghandi)

Our Acknowledgements

To all the marvellous contributors who have entered into the spirit of this book, and have unselfishly shared their lovely pets with us.

To dear friend Michael Heath for his, as ever, spontaneous humour.

To our publisher for her enthusiasm and encouragement.

And to You, for buying the book, thereby joining our efforts to help the less fortunate animals in our society who cannot speak for themselves, and who via the R.S.P.C.A. will benefit from the sales of *All Gourmets Great and Small*. If you were to buy this book for a friend and your friend bought the book for another friend, and so on and so on...... It wouldn't be too long before our joint efforts made a really worthwhile impact.

Contents

★   ★   ★   ★   ★

Scrummy I: Starters

★   ★   ★   ★   ★

Scrummy II: Main Courses

★ ★ ★ ★ ★

Scrummy III: Afters

Introduction

During the course of writing *The Broad Oak Cookbook* and running a restaurant, we have, naturally, had left-overs. These are usually in greater variety than in the average household – some are the leafy trimmings that people leave so as not to appear famished, the bits they don't want to leave their teeth stuck in under the adoring gaze of the beloved, or the result of having "eyes bigger than stomach", as Mummy would say.

Our chickens never mind where these delicious "scraps" come from, and scuttle about the fields with various mayonnaise and piquant sauce-coated trophies, producing enormous, orange-yolked eggs.

We soon noticed that other animals were helping themselves to carefully selected morsels from the daily buckets – smoked prawn shells for the pony, with the occasional treat of a whole pineapple shell (missing only its sorbet filling), baked potatoes soaked in rich gravy, and red cabbage with garlic dip for the sheep. Chocolate brandy gateau and ratatouille were delicacies for the dog and cat.

We wondered how many other animals would enjoy a change from the normal dreary tin, given the chance, and our research has shown that many already do.

In this book we have put together some recipes, based on ideas kindly suggested by various international stars, politicians, writers etc., who share their busy lives with much-loved pets.

It will not teach you to cook – there are plenty of marvellous books that do that better than we could – but hopefully it will give you some ideas, and amuse you at the same time.

The idea is, from time to time, to use ingredients that you know your animal likes and either save a little of the raw material, or some of the finished article.

Animals like and need variety, just as we do. Don't assume just because your dog has never eaten lasagne verde that he'll hate it! (You'll certainly hate us if he sicks it up on the Persian rug, so try a little at a time to start with!)

When you are cooking, especially vegetables, why not do a little extra for the animals, added to what they already enjoy?

When your dog has had a busy day gnawing the postman, searching for prehistoric man beneath the rose bushes, or re-cycling your Gucci shoes, he does not want to come in and find you hunched over the tin-opener, night after night, murmuring "din-dins" over a plate of boiled brown pony.

Most of the recipes are inspired by dogs and cats, simply because they are the most common pets, and more adaptable to change, unlike racehorses or pythons, who have fairly fixed ideas and delicate digestions.

We have been delighted by the positive approach of our famous contributors, and we hope you will enjoy this peep into a little – but very important – corner of their lives.

We love the idea of Elaine Paige bothering to cook Tugger's meal with her own fair hands when she could so easily open a tin – or get someone else to – and Tugger would love her just the same; and the Chairman of I.C.I. with his dog asleep under his desk!

There is a growing conviction that animals are a positive health benefit. Dr Roger Mugford, a psychologist and expert in animal behaviour, says: "A lot of health professionals will tell you that animals act as therapists, keeping society happy in a quiet, unspoken way."

It has been argued that it is unnatural not to keep a pet. Lesley Scott-Ordish runs the Pro-Dog charity whose volunteers take nearly 3,000 dogs to visit the elderly, children and mental patients in homes and hospitals around the country – "People who are so withdrawn they can hardly speak to anyone will respond to an animal". You will probably have your own favourite animal charity – there are lots to choose from, and a few are mentioned at the back of this book. In a world increasingly full of human disasters, animal charities often find themselves way down the line when it comes to much-needed support. In view of the valuable part animals play in our lives, this seems unfair.

The R.S.P.C.A., whose patron is H.M. Queen Elizabeth The Queen Mother, will benefit from the sales of *All Gourmets Great and Small*. If you have already bought the book you have helped – for which, on behalf of the animals, thank you.

★   ★   ★   ★   ★

2

Dog Dynasty

We have our own little "dog dynasty" — Sam, his daughter Alice, and her son, Tips.

We'd love to hear about other families, and wonder what the largest family is and whether they are still in touch with one another? (We exclude pedigrees from our enquiries, as obviously these can be traced for many generations).

Sadly, Sam and Alice are no longer with us, but Tips does still see his Auntie Daisy from time to time.

Sam Watson was one of the all-time canine characters and the father and grandfather of our two almost-whippets, or "snippets". He was closely related to a countless variety of other dogs — often unbeknown to their owners and frequently to their horror. He travelled many dangerous miles in his quest to perpetuate his remarkable line, and expected a decent meal at whatever time he chose to return from his family planning trips. Fortunately, he would eat most things, but he was very fond of salad (a taste passed on to his grandson), and was a well-known spaghetti sucker.

Sam died dramatically and with maximum effect on December 25th, thus ensuring that Christmas lunch is now synonymous with the grief of his passing, and that, at the worst way, he will be remembered by the entire family at least once a year.

Alice was the result of an illicit union between a well bred whippet of advanced years and the legendary Sam. The marriage was consummated on the lawn in front of some rather horrified guests at a country house hotel. An elderly lady rushed to the proprietor saying, "There's a dead dog in the garden!", leading her to the exhausted, post-coital form of the wayward Minnie Mouse.

Alice became almost indistinguishable from a "real" whippet and a most beloved companion. She used to visit her father from time to time, and she inherited his love of continental food. A valued friend and customer in our restaurant always used to order an extra portion of mediterranean crevettes or prawns in garlic for Alice. He would even share his pastrami with his "little friend".

Tips, originally called Werewolf because of his greyish, faded coat, Sam's grandson, was born in a Welsh stable. We naively believed that Alice wasn't "that kind of girl" until she succumbed to the fatal charm of the lovesick sheepdog who slept under our window all night in a snowstorm.

Tips (or Gratuities as he was often called) is a strange and loving little character with a little of all his known ancestors clearly visible. He is very nearly a vegetarian, and loves curry, chilli, salad, pasta, and above all, banana. There are

Our own little Dog Dynasty

Alice

Tips

Sam

few, if any, recipes in this book that he would not enjoy.

Luckily, he is not awfully keen on what he regards as the slightly mucky business of reproduction – apart from the three-legged tart from the bungalow.

Indiscriminate breeding – although we have joked about Sam and his exploits – leads to a great deal of unhappiness, especially for the animals. Literally thousands of dogs alone are destroyed *per week* because they are unwanted. This applies to other species of animals too, and could so easily be avoided. We don't want to get into the gigantic subject of cruelty, vivisection, zoos, vegetarianism – you will have your own views and the charities mentioned in this book will be delighted to advise you.

All we do want to say is that if you do think of adding an animal to your family, please give a home to someone already longing for a bit of the love and respect he, she or it deserves. Battersea Dogs Home is bursting with them for a start!

We made the fatal mistake of "ordering" an unborn (unconceived even!) puppy. Quelle disaster!

What we got was a piece of diabolical genetic engineering, the runt of a litter of one. A canine Ghengis Khan, delivered, screaming, in a plastic suitcase. He was everything ghastly in an animal, but we loved him just the same. Unfortunately, he had a deep fondness for lamb – preferably alive and if possible, mobile. We still have the scratches on our television from his attempts to enter the set during "One Man and His Dog". How Pip longed with all his little black heart to be that dog!

This is not a cookbook for animals, and we don't suggest for one moment that you abandon tinned food altogether – some of it is very good and well-balanced (despite appearances!), although we have heard of a dog who won't touch his normal brand of tinned food when it is on special offer. Can he really read the price, or is it inferior quality and not a special offer after all?

All Gourmets Great and Small is just an ideas book for all of us, with them in mind, and we're not suggesting that you humanise your animals!

★   ★   ★   ★   ★

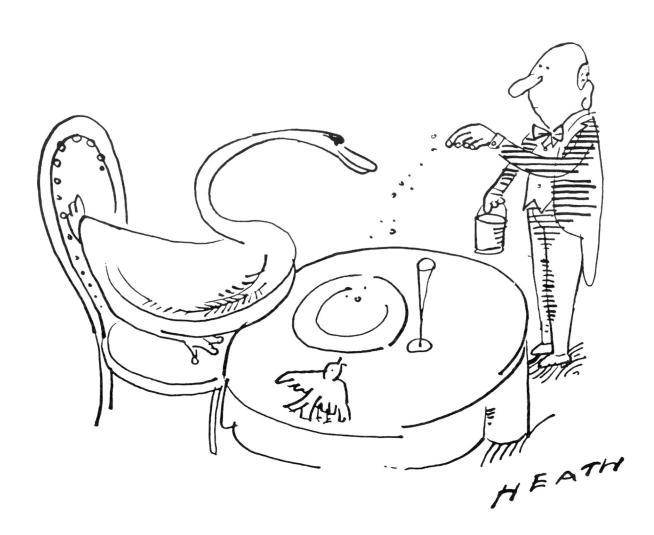

HEATH

★ ★ ★ ★ ★ ★ ★

Scrummy I: STARTERS

★ ★ ★ ★ ★ ★ ★

Katie Boyle

For many years Katie Boyle has been one of our most popular and glamorous television personalities. She has always had dogs around her, ever since her Italian childhood, and she remembers that in Italy they used to cut out a lot of red meat in the animals' diet, replacing it with chicken or fish, and mixing it with cooked rice and grated raw carrot.

Katie doesn't just talk about her fondness for animals, she is actively involved in their welfare, being on the committee of Battersea Dogs Home. She does use some tinned food – but laced with chicken or fish, and topped up in the winter with a few drops of Abidec, a childrens' vitamin complex. In the summer her dogs appreciate their grated raw carrot or chopped raw spinach, mixed in with the former combination. Extra treats consist of baked liver, small hearts and boiled chicken livers.

Both Katie's dogs are "rescuees" – Baba has a savoury tooth, and camembert is her caviar, whilst Bizzie (who has to watch her weight!) much prefers soft Italian chocolates called Gianduiottis.

This recipe for pâté is a good excuse to buy some chicken livers for the dogs. They might even like the taste of the finished product.

Chicken Liver and Herb Pâté
(with hot chutney)

2 tablespoons walnut oil
1 onion (finely chopped)
1lb/500g chicken livers
1 tablespoon chopped fresh parsley
1 tcaspoon chopped fresh thyme

1 teaspoon chopped fresh sage
2 cloves garlic (crushed)
2 tablespoons brandy
salt and black pepper

- Fry the onion in the walnut oil until just soft. Add the chicken livers and herbs and fry for a few minutes, until the livers just lose their pinkness. Liquidize, adding the seasoning and brandy, until smooth.
- Spoon the mixture into an earthenware terrine and chill for a least two hours – preferably overnight.
- Serve with hot toast and a tiny touch of the following hot chutney, which comes via a Mr Tsai from Hong Kong.

★ ★ ★ ★ ★

Very Hot Chutney

1lb/500g tin of tomatoes
1 inch fresh ginger
2 cloves garlic (crushed)
1 teaspoon hot chilli powder

4oz/115g brown sugar
4oz/115g stoned plums
2 tablespoons vinegar

- First chop the ginger and plums very finely, and smash the tomatoes well.
- Put your vessel on the fire, and add a small cup of oil. Don't let the oil burn too long – when just hot, put in the ginger and then the chilli powder, garlic, plums and tomatoes, lowering the flame as you do so. Add the vinegar, sugar and a pinch of salt. Keep the fire low, stirring gently now and again.
- When the tomatoes are well smashed, the oil will come up and it gets quite thickish. Remove from the fire, taste for hotness, and if need be add more chilli and sugar.
- Bottle and store in a cool place.
- This is Mr Tsai's recipe almost word for word – don't hesitate to contact him in Hong Kong if you have any queries.

Carla Lane

Although Carla Lane lives in London, she manages to share her life with a variety of animals – rabbits, guinea-pigs, four cats, a wolfhound, thirty-six birds and two tortoises! All the cats adore avocado and will jump high in the air for a piece.

The quiet, devious escapologist "Danielle" loves avocado on toast more than anything in the world.

Wolfgang, the five-year old ginger "boss-cat", likes cottage cheese with pineapple. Pandora – a female villain – loves Flora on all her food, and the shy Sorrow must have goldfish food sprinkled over everything. None of them like milk – they prefer melted ice-cream. Maximus, the wolfhound, likes bananas better than bones and eats a pot of honey a week.

The tortoises have baby food, preferably spinach, and apple and banana dessert.

All the birds love fresh pea-pods and cucumber, and the rabbits and guinea-pigs have a mixture of muesli and parrot food.

It is amazing that Carla ever finds time to write, with all these creatures around her, but she loves all animals dearly. Maybe that is why she gave such a good part to "Mongey" in "Bread", one of her greatest T.V. successes.

While she is buying avocados by the box, she deserves a little up market treat herself – avocado on toast for the cats, but "Avocado Crunchies" for Carla:

Avocado Crunchies

4 long brown rolls (approx 6")
2 ripe avocados
4 spring onions (finely chopped)
1 chilli pepper (seeded & finely chopped)
2 tablespoons fresh lemon or lime juice
2 teaspoons cumin powder
1 garlic clove (crushed)
1 tomato (peeled and chopped)
1 teaspoon Tabasco sauce
1 teaspoon Worcester sauce
1 tablespoon olive oil
Parmesan cheese
salt and pepper

- Slice the tops from the rolls horizontally. Scoop out the dough and grate into breadcrumbs.
- Mash together the avocado, onions, tomato, chilli, lemon juice, garlic and cumin. Add the Tabasco, Worcester sauce, and salt and pepper to taste. Blend in the breadcrumbs.
- Put the bread shells on a baking tray and drizzle over the olive oil. Fill with the avocado mixture. Sprinkle with a little grated Parmesan and bake in a pre-heated oven gas 7 (425°F) for about 15 minutes, or until brown and bubbling. (It may be necessary to add the Parmesan halfway through baking, as it is apt to burn easily.)

★　★　★　★　★

Sir
Michael Hordern

We were delighted to hear from Sir Michael Hordern, who is one of our favourite actors. Although he has no animals now, as he lives in London, he remembers a boyhood companion, named "Treacle Tart", who was known to help in the picking of whortleberries (or blueberries) on Dartmoor. Treacle Tart also ate the berries and appeared to enjoy them.

Sadly, he has been gone some fifty-five years, and left no photographs. He is not forgotten and somehow we can picture him, snuffling among the heather, with his little teeth stained in a blueberry smile!

Whortleberries are delicious in pies or pancakes, and also make tasty and very attractive ice cream and sorbet. Our recipe is something a little different – it must be served very cold.

12

Treacle Tart Soup

1 1/2lb/700g fresh ripe blueberries
8oz/225g grapes
4fl.oz/100ml single cream
4fl.oz/100ml natural yoghurt
2 teaspoons fresh lemon juice
1/4 teaspoon sugar
1/2 pint/200ml Perrier water

- Wash and generally tidy up the blueberries. Chill all the ingredients (except the sugar) until just before using. Put the soup bowls into the freezer. Puree the fruit in the food processor. Strain the pulp through a wire sieve. Stir in the remaining ingredients, leaving the Perrier water until last. Serve at once in the chilled bowls.

★   ★   ★   ★   ★

Sylvia Syms

Animals are reputed to be soothing and to help keep you young – this could be Sylvia Syms' secret! Her stage and film career has spanned many years – it's hard to believe that back in the 1950's her "lust-in-the-dust" love scene with John Mills, in "Ice Cold in Alex", was edited out for being too steamy!

Sylvia Syms has an elderly Jack Russell called "Snoopy", who enjoys Stilton (although the resulting whiffs can be a bit off-putting!) and Molly, a Sheltie. Her dogs have little meat, and quite a lot of brown rice and pasta, which she cooks with Bovril or Marmite flavoured water. This is mixed with liver, boned turkey legs and minced scraps.

Pasta is a wonderful standby. We all at some time have had to face a devoted, ravenous pet, knowing that the cupboard is bare, due to our inefficiency or laziness; but if animals are used to a little variety, you need never be caught out.

Stilton is no longer brought out only at Christmas. It finds itself in all sorts of strange places these days; stuffed into fruit, deep-fried and chilled.

In Sylvia Syms' house it finds its way into Snoopy – here's a little treat that all can enjoy, and Snoopy gets the left-overs!

★ ★ ★ ★ ★

Snoopy's Stilton Cream

1pint/20fl.oz double cream
8oz/170g stilton (crumbled)
6 medium eggs
1 clove garlic (crushed)
1/2 teaspoon tabasco sauce
black pepper

- In a processor blend the cheese, garlic, eggs, pepper and tabasco until smooth. Add the cream and blend again. Pour into buttered ramekins and place on an oven tray. Bake in a pre-heated oven gas 5 (375°F) for 30 minutes until just set.

★ ★ ★ ★ ★

Patrick Moore
O.B.E.

As an astronomer, Patrick Moore is very much a nocturnal creature himself, and you would therefore expect him to favour cats.

His little black and white companion, "Bonnie", is probably delighted when her master sits up all night watching the stars! Bonnie loves haddock, and this, word for word of course, is how Patrick cooks it for her:

"Take a haddock fillet. Pour over it, in a saucepan, boiling water (it must be boiling). Leave it for 2–3 minutes. Then take it out of the saucepan, put it on a plate, chop it up (she likes it rather fine), leave a minute to cool, and put it down for her. This is always greeted with a contented purr. Conclude the meal by a saucer of creamy milk!"

Our recipe is for a soft fishy pâté – Bonnie might even like this, but it certainly gives an excuse to buy some extra haddock.

★   ★   ★   ★   ★

Pâté Bonnie-Cat

1lb/500g fresh haddock
5fl.oz/150ml olive oil
Juice of 2 lemons
3 cloves garlic (crushed)
2 tablespoons fresh white breadcrumbs
5fl.oz/150ml double cream
salt and black pepper

- Fillet the haddock and cut into chunks. Put the fish and the oil into a heavy saucepan, and cook gently until the fish is very soft. Gradually stir in the garlic, lemon juice and seasoning. Remove from the heat and beat in the cream and the breadcrumbs. Either continue beating, or process until smooth.
- Put into an ovenproof dish and bake at gas 6 (400°F) for about 40 minutes, or until the top is brown and crunchy. Allow to cool. When firm, turn out and serve with fried bread or toast.

☆ ☆ ☆ Bill Waddington ☆ ☆ ☆

From the moment he joined the characters in television's longest running soap opera, "Coronation Street", the officious know-all, "Percy Sugden" has managed at some time to rub almost everyone up the wrong way!

In real life, however, you couldn't wish to meet a kinder, more considerate man than Bill Waddington, who has eight much-loved racehorses, one of which rejoices in the name "Lottie Limejuice".

Bill is unable to keep animals in his flat, but he shares his daughter's three dogs and five cats.

"I did have a fox terrier dog who loved an orange and pickled onions. He was different to any dog I ever had; people used to be so amused by him and his queer diet". Bill Waddington even once kept a pet turkey named "Eric", who appeared as the star guest on Bill's delightful "This is Your Life".

Here is a delicious orangey soup, which we think Bill's Fox Terrier would have approved of!

Rover's Return Again Soup

1lb/$^1/_2$ kilo courgettes
1 medium onion (thinly sliced)
1oz/25g butter
1 teaspoon chopped fresh basil
5fl.oz/150ml single cream
grated rind of 1 large orange
3fl.oz/75ml fresh orange juice
2oz/55g brown rice
2pts/1.1 litre water

- Cook the rice in plenty of water while you are preparing the soup –
  brown rice takes longer than white.
- Wash the courgettes, trim both ends and slice roughly. Soften the
  onion in the butter. Add the courgettes and the basil, cover the pan
  and cook gently for about 10 mins. Add the water, bring to the boil
  and simmer until the courgettes are tender – about – 10 minutes.
- Liquidize and then add the cream, orange juice and orange rind,
  and season to taste. Drain the rice, rinse and keep warm. As soon as
  the soup is ready, divide the rice between four bowls and pour the
  soup over. Serve with fried croutons.

(NB For a special treat – but definitely NOT for the doggie bag! – add a
spoonful of orange wine to each portion.)

★   ★   ★   ★   ★

During his touring days Ernie had a brindle Scottie called "Hannibal Boots", who used to like Heinz strained carrots mixed with his biscuits – and he loved onions.

Ernie's beloved poodle, "Charlie", lived for twelve years on a diet of raw mince and Brie. Every time Ernie took a cheque out of the book, Charlie used to howl. He was also terrified of thunder and young children – altogether a very smart dog!

Ernie Wise now has a cat who enjoys scrambled egg with cheese, spaghetti sauce, and curry. Here's a spicy version for the whole family.

Persian Scrambled Eggs

1 onion (chopped finely)
2 tomatoes (skinned and quartered)
1 teaspoon grated root ginger
2 green chillies (chopped and seeded)
1 tablespoon chopped fresh coriander leaves (use another fresh herb if you can't manage coriander)
2oz/50g unsalted butter
pinch ground turmeric
1/2 teaspoon ground cumin
6 eggs
black pepper

- Heat the butter in a heavy pan. Fry the onion until just brown. Add all the ingredients (except the eggs), and continue cooking for a further 5 minutes.
- Keep warm, while scrambling the eggs with a little butter. Put the eggs on top of the spicy mixture and serve with, but not on, hot toast.

The number this will feed depends entirely upon how greedy or stingy the cook is, and if your cat is anything like Ernie Wise's he'll probably help you out!

★   ★   ★   ★   ★

Sir John Mills

The famous and richly talented "theatrical family Mills" love animals and at one time even owned a farm in Sussex. It was here that the decision was made to cast the twelve-year-old pony-mad Hayley in her first remarkable film, "Tiger Bay" – for which we should all be truly thankful! Sir John and Lady Mills now have a Yorkshire terrier, "Mr. Chips", who is passionately fond of Norwegian goats' cheese, with which Sir John invariably finishes lunch. "He is quite happy to lie quietly in a corner while we are eating, but as soon as he sees the small red box appear he immediately sits up and begs, saying 'please' very quietly until he gets some!"

Mr Chips is famous in his own right as, helped by Lady Mills (the writer, Mary Hayley Bell), he wrote his own story in a book called *Him, Her and Me*, published by Weidenfeld.

Goats' cheese has a definite flavour and is becoming much more available, especially as quite a few sheep farmers are switching to goats. Goats' milk is very much easier to digest than cows' milk and is useful for sickly animals, as well as humans. Even some horses drink it.

★ ★ ★ ★ ★

Goats' Cheese Pancakes

3oz/85g goats' cheese
3fl.oz/75ml sour cream (if you can't buy it easily, make your own with
a 50/50 mixture of double cream and plain yoghurt)
2oz/55g plain flour
1/2 teaspoon salt
3 large eggs
melted unsalted butter

- In a bowl, or food processor, blend all the ingredients thoroughly.
- Heat a heavy pan and brush with the melted butter.
- Drop the mixture in spoonfuls into the hot pan.
- Cook slowly until bubbles burst. Turn and cook the other side until brown.
- Brush with melted butter, keep warm, and serve with maple syrup.

Can be served as the beginning of a meal, with perhaps a more savoury sauce.

✦ ☆ ☆ Diana Rigg C.B.E. ☆ ☆ ✦

W hatever else she does, Diana Rigg will always be remembered for her portrayal of Emma Peel, although she has changed her image slightly from those leather-clad "Avenger" days!

She spends a good deal of time in Scotland and has several dogs.

"By far the most gluttonous is a much-loved Springer Spaniel who will eat anything. She is not only a glutton, but a whore, a thief and a coward. Called Lily, but known as "Fireside Lil" for obvious reasons."

Well, "Fireside Lil" looks as though butter wouldn't melt in her greedy little mouth, but nevertheless, the recipe just has to be a tart of some sort! We thought this might be tasty – if you could get to it before Lily – washed down with a little chilled Chablis.

Lily's Fireside Tartlets

For the pastry:

8oz/225g plain flour
2oz/55g butter or margarine
2oz/55g lard
2 teaspoons chopped fresh fennel leaves

For the filling:

1 medium onion (finely sliced)
knob of butter
8oz/250g chopped flesh of Mediterranean
   crevettes/Dublin Bay prawns or lobster claws
2 teaspoons chopped fresh parsley
2 tablespoons double cream
4oz/115g cream cheese (softened)
2oz/55g unpeeled prawns for garnish
black pepper

- Make the pastry as usual, and add the fennel.
- Roll out and line individual buttered tart tins. Prick the bases and bake blind for approximately 10 minutes at gas 6 (400°F). Remove when pastry forms a slight crust. Fry the onion gently in the butter until soft. Remove from the heat and stir in the fish, cheese, cream, most of the parsley and a generous grind of black pepper. Spoon the mixture into the cases and bake in an oven gas 4 (305°F) for about 20 minutes or until the filling is just set.
- Decorate each little tart with a whole unpeeled prawn and a sprinkling of the remaining parsley.

★ ★ ★ ★ ★

Christina Foyle owns what is arguably the world's most famous bookshop. She has ten cats, and her Siamese, "Mimi", has been chosen to give his favourite recipe for a deluxe pâté, which consists of minced cooked rabbit, liver and chicken, with 3 tablespoons of Whiskas to give it body. Serve cold.

Mimi is prepared to attend signing sessions, or even make an author's tour when necessary. These literary occasions can be exhausting, and stimulating refreshments are the order of the day. While the champagne is being pawed, we are sure that Mimi will like to nibble on these special "Mimibix". We have never known a Siamese who didn't favour the finer things in life. They often love travelling – our "Mr Moto" went everywhere in my father's car, draped over his shoulders like a fox fur. In those days, of course, the man had only just stopped walking in front with a red flag so it wasn't quite as dangerous. A neighbour drove everywhere with a large goose beside him – but then he did actually drop dead at the wheel – luckily no harm came to anyone, least of all the goose!

Mimibix

4oz/115g self-raising flour
2oz/60g unsalted butter
2oz/60g smoked salmon (finely minced)
4fl.oz/120ml thick cream
2fl.oz/60ml sour cream
2 tablespoons milk
4 tablespoons salmon roe

- Sift the flour with a pinch of salt. Dice the butter and blend with the flour until the mixture is like breadcrumbs. Add the smoked salmon and sufficient of the cream to make a soft dough. Roll out the dough on a lightly floured board until it is about 1/2 inch thick.
- Cut into small shapes and put on a baking tray. Chill. Brush lightly with milk and bake in a pre-heated oven gas 6 (400°F) for about 15 minutes or until they are golden and puffed up.
- Halve the biscuits horizontally and allow to cool. Spoon sour cream on to each and top with some salmon roe. Sprinkle with a little finely chopped fennel or dill. Makes a yummy little cocktail snack.

★ ★ ★ ★ ★

Jilly is the beautiful and successful author of countless un-put-downable books. Don't be misled by the picture of her relaxing with her loved ones – she is amazingly hard-working, and it is probably just as well that her animals enjoy their chicken well cooked, as she certainly doesn't have time to crouch over the Aga prodding breasts and thighs all day.

Although her beloved mongrel, Fortnum, is now free to roam the great big Common in the Sky, his beautiful daughters, Mabel and Barbara, live on.

They enjoy their well cooked chicken with plenty of garlic. Another favourite is ox liver or heart, chopped up into bite-sized pieces, cooked in chicken stock made with two stock cubes, lots of garlic, in a hot oven for an hour.

Our recipe uses up Mabel and Barbaras chicken left-overs – you may already have a favourite way of making chicken soup, but it certainly won't be easier than ours!

Chicken Soup With Puff Pastry

When you and your animals have eaten all you want of the roast chicken, empty the entire contents of the roasting tin (complete with carcass, skin, jelly, shrivelled-up cloves of garlic, halves of lemon, stuffing, cremated herbs and anything else you have inserted into the hapless bird) into a large saucepan.

- Cover with cold water. Add a chopped carrot, a small onion or leek, and some chopped celery. Cover and bring to the boil, then simmer for 1 1/2–2 hours or longer. Strain and allow to cool. Remove the fat. Re-heat and add seasoning. You can thicken it up with cream, cook some barley or rice in it, or puree some cooked vegetables and stir that in. A splosh of sherry is always well received.

- Approximately 1 pound of puff pastry should be enough for four. Choose deep soup bowls, and cut out four rounds of pastry with a generous overhang. Divide the soup among the bowls. Brush one side of the pastry all round the edge with beaten egg, and press firmly on to the bowl. Put the bowls carefully into the fridge for at least an hour.

- Pre-heat the oven to gas 8 (450°F). Brush the tops of the pastry lids with egg wash, put the bowls onto a baking tray and bake for approximately 15 minutes. Serve at once. (Don't forget to keep your bits of left-over pastry to make some home-made dog bikkies. See page 97.)

★　★　★　★　★

 # Una Stubbs

Una Stubbs' pets are robins. During the winter she feeds them daily with moist bread, nuts, fat and water. During the spring she moves the food to near the door (except the nuts). Then the food is put inside the house by the door. As the weather improves she stops putting the food out, and lets "the darlings" wander around, picking up the children's crumbs.

Robins are delightful, friendly creatures, gentle, lively and lovely to watch – a lot like Una herself. Looking at her now, it is hard to believe that she made a film with Cliff Richard back in the days when he still curled his lip and greased his hair. She is still Alf Garnett's daughter, and prances about in "Give Us A Clue".

Katie Boyle suggests collecting berries when they are plentiful and freezing them – remember to label them carefully! You then have a free emergency supply for the harsh winter months when so many birds starve.

People who love animals will always find a way of being with them, even if they cannot keep a conventional pet for some reason or other, and to have the trust of a truly wild creature is perhaps the greatest compliment.

George Cole

☆ ☆ ☆   ★ ☆ ☆

Long before the heady days of Arthur Daley, George Cole had a cat who lived for eighteen years, and had a penchant for baked beans. As we all know, the effects of this delicacy can be devastatingly antisocial. Frank obviously either lived outside or blamed it on someone else.

Home-made baked beans beat the tinned variety into a cocked hat, although they do take just a little longer to prepare! This is a hotted up version, so if you have a bean-loving four-legged pal, we suggest you go easy on the chilli powder.

★   ★   ★   ★   ★

Frank's Beano

1lb/500g haricot beans
4 slices of streaky bacon
2 small onions
2 tablespoons English mustard
2 tablespoons black treacle
2 tablespoons soft dark brown sugar
1 teaspoon salt
1 teaspoon chilli powder

- Soak the beans overnight in cold water. Drain and put into a saucepan with enough water to cover by an inch. Simmer for 1 1/2 hours until the skins just start to burst and the beans are tender. Drain.
- Cut the bacon into 1 inch strips and fry.
- Put the beans, and fried bacon (and its juices) into a deep earthernware casserole. Push the onions down either side.
- Mix the other ingredients with a teacup of boiling water and pour over the beans. Add enough boiling water to just cover, and cook at gas 2 (300°F), or lower, for 5–6 hours, leaving the pot uncovered for the last 2 hours. Add more boiling water if necessary. Serve with warm granary bread.

★   ★   ★   ★   ★

☆ ☆ ☆ **Brigitte Bardot** ☆ ☆ ☆

Brigitte has loved all animals since childhood, and has been nicknamed "The Madonna of the Strays". She campaigned vigorously and successfully on behalf of the baby seals being slaughtered in Newfoundland, and achieved changes (known as "The B.B. Law") in the rules regulating French abattoirs.

She recently sold most of her jewels and the souvenirs of her remarkable career in order to create a charitable trust devoted to animals, and says that she's had more mail – much of it from the young – than she ever had at the height of her "sex kitten" fame!

Roger Vadim "freed" the young Brigitte from the confines of her respectable Paris family. Now she has set herself free from the trappings of stardom to live her life for her animals.

Oeufs Brigitte

Of course our recipe for Brigitte must be vegetarian, and so we've chosen a simple but delicious starter or snack, using the eggs of Bantam chickens. These are delightful, colourful little characters, fun to have around and beautiful to look at, especially the cockerels.

For 4 people:

4 Bantam eggs
2 ripe avocadoes
8 stoned black olives (chopped)
4 tablespoons home-made mayonnaise
1 teaspoon tomato ketchup
black pepper

- Combine the mayonnaise and the ketchup. Halve and stone the avocadoes and rub the surface with a little lemon juice to avoid browning. Put each half into a small dish, specially shaped if possible.
- Poach the bantam eggs in a saucepan of boiling water to which a little vinegar has been added. Remove with a slotted spoon and tidy up the edges.
- Place an egg in each pear half, and spoon a little ribbon of mayonnaise around the inner edge of the avocado. Grind black pepper over the eggs and decorate with chopped olive. Serve avec toast soldiers (or matelots or whatever you fancy!).

Bryan Forbes

and
Nanette Newman

Bryan Forbes and his wife, Nanette Newman, have worked together during their long-running film careers. They still do so, but in addition to this they have branched out into the worlds of writing and publishing – even owning their own bookshop. Despite their great success, they remain natural and charming, resisting the temptations of tax-free life abroad to remain in England.

Nanette has written several cookbooks herself, so we are treading very carefully!

The Forbes household has a large menagerie and a whole posse of cats with amazing culinary tastes. They enjoy a wide variety of foods and, in particular during the summer months, have a great liking for melon. They will not only fastidiously eat the pulp, but go on to eat the shell as well. They also love salads, and will eat tomatoes. There appears to be no food that they won't at some time sample. The mother cat has a particular fondness for salted peanuts.

We think these tastes combine surprisingly well, and make a rather unique starter.

★　★　★　★　★

Melon With Peanut Sauce

1 ripe melon
4 large firm tomatoes (peeled and seeded)
4oz/115g peanut butter
3fl.oz/75ml strong chicken stock
2fl.oz/50ml soy sauce
3fl.oz/75ml sesame oil
2 cloves garlic (crushed)
1 tablespoon fresh ginger root (peeled and grated)
1 tablespoon sugar
2 tablespoon wine vinegar
1 teaspoon paprika
2fl.oz/50ml double cream

- Put all the ingredients, except the tomatoes, the melon and the cream, into the processor, and blend until smooth. Continue to blend, and gradually add the cream. Remove the flesh from the melon and cut into chunks. Roughly chop the tomatoes.
- Put into individual glasses and chill. Just before serving, pour over a little of the sauce and garnish with a few chopped peanuts and a little chopped parsley.

★　★　★　★　★

☆ ☆ ☆ Ken Livingstone ☆ ☆ ☆

The M.P. Ken Livingstone – or "Citizen Ken" as he has been called – is very fond of animals, especially amphibious reptiles, who enjoy dishes which include lots of water and live scrunchy things.

Well, scrunchy we can do, and we suggest perhaps white Sangria to wash it all down, but we draw the line at the live part!

Politics appears to have been a second choice for Mr Livingstone, who originally wanted to work in the zoo.

As a child, he created a steamy jungle atmosphere in his bedroom, surrounded by a variety of unattractive reptiles and creepy crawlies. Obviously, he is well prepared for life in the corridors of power!

We have suggested some crunchy nibbles, two of them with a definite red tinge, which could be served as hors d'oeuvres for a "croctail" party.

★ ★ ★ ★ ★

Snail Tarts:

12 1inch slices of slender
   French bread
12 big snails (rinsed and fried)
4fl.oz/100ml dry white wine
4fl.oz/100ml chicken stock
2 shallots (finely chopped)
2 cloves garlic (minced)

1 teaspoon of fresh chopped thyme
3 tablespoons chopped fresh parsley
1 teaspoon fresh lemon juice
4fl.oz/100ml thick cream
salt & pepper

- Hollow out the dough from the bread slices, leaving a base. Brush with melted butter and bake for about 10 minutes or until golden brown. Cool on a rack.
- Combine the snails, wine, stock, lemon juice, shallots, garlic and thyme, and cook over a high heat until the liquid is reduced to about 3 tablespoons. Add the cream and 2 tablespoons of the parsley, season with salt and pepper, and reduce the liquid again to about 4 tablespoons. Put a snail in each case, add some sauce and garnish with the remaining parsley.

★　★　★　★　★

Stuffed Red Radishes:

2 bunches of big red radishes (washed)
4oz/115g butter
4oz/115g Stilton or other strong blue cheese
Process the butter and the cheese until smooth and soft.

- Slice the base of each radish so that it stands. With a melonball cutter scoop out a hole from the other end.
- Chill the radishes in iced water, and drain before using.
- Pipe in the mixture and chill again. Sprinkle with chopped chives before serving.

★　★　★　★　★

Deep-fried Strawberries:

1lb/450g fresh firm English strawberries
Batter (see page 37, Crispy Celery Leaves)
Caster sugar

- Rinse but don't hull the strawberries. Drain and dry on kitchen paper. Dip the strawberries in the batter and deep-fry until crisp. Drain on kitchen paper and roll in the sugar.

✩ ✩ ✩ **Beryl Reid O.B.E.** ✩ ✩ ✩

It would be impossible to do justice here to Beryl Reid's stage, film, television and radio career. Our personal maxim is that "if Beryl's in it, it's going to be good", and a particular favourite that springs to mind is the eccentric Scottish Madame Arcati in a revival of Noel Coward's "Blithe Spirit". But we all have our favourites – we mustn't forget "Marlene" – and luckily Beryl Reid gives us a wealth to choose from.

She lives on the banks of the Thames with her family of around ten cats at any one time. She says that they are very fond of lasagne verde, and adore garlic. They also enjoy cheese, and there was one who ate cabbage stalks and rose petals! There are limited recipes using roses, so we suggest a small flower arrangement on the table from which pussy can help himself – rather like After Eights. This will give more pleasure, as it will have the element of naughtiness. Beryl not only loves cats, but understands and respects them too. Her recent book "Cats Whiskers" is a treasure trove of amusing and moving stories about her own and other peoples pussies – well worth a read.

Garlic is a very valuable addition to a human as well as an animal diet, and many of our recipes already contain it. Here is one for soup, which makes a wonderful late snack on a chilly night – ideal for keeping colds and Draculas at bay.

★ ★ ★ ★ ★

Garlic Soup

4 thick slices of French bread
olive oil (best, not Shell Multigrade)
10 cloves of garlic (crushed)
35fl.oz/1 litre chicken stock

- Brush the bread with olive oil on both sides and put on a baking tray in a pre-heated oven gas 4 (350°F) until brown and crisp — approximately 20 minutes.
- Gently cook the garlic in some olive oil, without letting it brown. Pour in the chicken stock and bring to the boil. Simmer for about 5 minutes. Put a piece of bread in each bowl and pour on the soup.

★　★　★　★　★

Crispy Celery Leaves

tops from 2 bunches of celery
6fl.oz/175ml milk
1 large egg
1 tablespoon melted butter
4oz/115g flour
1/2 teaspoon salt
1oz/30g Stilton cheese (finely crumbled)

- Clean the celery leaves and shake them dry. Mix together all but the cheese to make a smooth batter. Stir in the Stilton. Dip the celery in the batter, shake off the surplus, and then deep fry until golden brown. Drain on kitchen paper.

This makes a lovely cocktail snack. Do make sure that you snip the celery leaves into bite-sized pieces, and that you don't pulverise it into nothingness when you shake it dry.

And please, no clever experiments with other leaves from the garden, as poisoning causes lots of very embarrassing writhing about.

★　★　★　★　★

☆ ☆ ☆ **Dame Judi Dench** ☆ ☆ ☆

Judi Dench has had a distinguished theatrical career during which she has played most of the leading roles, including a remarkable Lady Macbeth, and St. Joan.

Despite all this success in a fantasy world, she is very much down-to-earth, with a great love of life and a sense of humour. She loves just being with her family, in which animals play an important part.

They once had a hampster with a penchant for cereals. Returning home from an anniversary celebration, Judi found the little creature with what appeared to be a broken leg, the bone sticking right through the skin. Distraught, Judi called the vet who removed the offending "bone". It turned out to be a sugar puff stuck to the hampster's fur!

The delightful "pussy-in-the-pot" picture is of Purwin Fosselton (almost named after a character in Mr & Mrs Nobody). There are three other cats — Newps, Spider and Tabs.

Henry is the dog, Letis is the rabbit, and the donkeys are Cal and Snowy.

Prawns and cheese occasionally feature on the menu, so we decided on an aprés-theatre snack, combining the two.

★ ★ ★ ★ ★

Garlic Prawns With Parsley Toast

Best cooked in a microwave — adjust timings to suit your own oven guide. Something is seriously wrong if this takes more than 10 minutes from freezer to hungry mouth. It is a good idea to make the butters in quantity and store in the 'fridge.

★ ★ ★ ★ ★

Garlic butter:

To each 8oz/225g butter or margarine add 2 cloves of crushed garlic, 1 teaspoon mixed dried herbs and some black pepper.

Parsley butter:

8oz/225g butter or margarine
2 tablespoons chooped fresh parsley
2 teaspoons Dijon mustard

To serve 2:

6oz/170g frozen peeled prawns
Garlic butter (as above)
Parsley butter (as above)
Four slices of white bread (crusts removed)
Parmesan cheese

- Pop prawns in microwave until ice has just melted.
- Drain and rest (the prawns!). Meanwhile, spread both sides of the bread with the parsley butter and bake in a pre-heated oven Gas 6 (400°F) for about 5 minutes or until golden brown.
- Divide prawns between two ramekins, add a generous knob of garlic butter and pop back in until just bubbling. DO NOT OVERCOOK unless you have a rubber fetish. Sprinkle a little Parmesan cheese on top and serve at once, accompanied by the parsley toast.

Bunny Roger

Bunny Roger, who lives and entertains in some style and splendour in London and at his home in Scotland, is one of a fast-fading breed of true characters. He was a leading designer for Fortnum and Mason's and for Hardy Amies and is a famous party-giver. If there isn't a special occasion he invents one, although his gatherings are a little more subdued these days. Anyone who can devise an amethyst jubilee just because he likes mauve has got to have some fun left in him, n'est'ce pas?

Bunny Roger's ravishingly beautiful cat, "Mary", never stops eating and "lives mainly on chopped raw beef – not really a staggering diet". She does, however, like chocolate, chocolate pudding, asparagus and melon. We've chosen something to use up the asparagus Mary discards, and we even make so bold as to suggest tinned asparagus, which Mary would probably throw straight in the bin without opening! If you can afford it, and if you can bring yourself to mangle up fresh asparagus, then by all means, do it! Fresh asparagus, incidentally, can also be baked, which is handy to know if you don't have an asparagus saucepan – such people really do exist, and not a million miles from here! Just chop off the woody ends and peel. Rinse drain and wrap in foil, sealing well. Bake at gas 7 (425°F) for 30 minutes or until tender.

Cheese and Asparagus Profiteroles

The filling:

8oz/250g cream cheese
1 tin of asparagus, well drained
juice of 1 lemon
black pepper

Blend all together in the liquidizer and chill.

Choux pastry:

4oz/115g butter
8fl.oz/250ml water
4oz/115g flour
4 eggs
pinch of salt

- Sift flour and salt on to a stiff piece of paper.
- Put butter and water into a saucepan and heat gently. When the butter melts, bring the water to the boil and tip in all the flour at once. Beat until smooth and leave to cool to blood heat.
- Whisk the eggs and gradually add to the mixture, beating thoroughly. You may not need all the eggs.
- Pipe or spoon on to a greased baking tray and bake in a pre-heated oven gas 5 (375°F) for 15–20 minutes. Cool on a rack. Poke little holes in the profiteroles and pipe in the asparagus mixture. Pile on a plate and serve as a starter or an unusual cocktail snack.

★ ★ ★ ★ ★

Pugs, despite their rotund little bodies, are associated with elegance – perhaps due to patronage by the Duchess of Windsor, who adored them, even having a row of pug-shaped cushions!. They may be regarded by some as lap-dogs, but they are brave and very amusing little characters and always fun to be with.

The internationally famous couturier, Valentino, who made Jacqueline Kennedy's dress for her wedding to Aristotle Onassis, and who designs for first ladies from all over the world – including Nancy Reagan – is passionately fond of his pug, "Oliver". So much so that he has named an entire menswear collection in his honour, with his name on every shirt label and jacket, his muzzle on buttons, belts and linings, and even the London boutique named after him. Could this "Oliver" ask for more?!

Mr. Valentino writes:

"The idea of your book is wonderful: it was about time that someone thought of gathering recipes for our little friends. I am delighted to give you one of Oliver's favourite dishes..."

★   ★   ★   ★   ★

Risotto à La Oliver

Boil white Arborio rice in vegetable broth, add some carrots and fresh green peas, and mix it with some previously cooked minced meat, and a spoonful of olive oil.

Stunningly simple – just like the best dress designs – we went a step further for ourselves (although our dog adored it both ways!) by adding the risotto to the chopped flesh of an aubergine, fried with a little tomato puree, basil and garlic. Replace in the aubergine "shells", sprinkle with a little Parmesan and some more oil and bake. Delicious cold, with a glass of your favourite Italian wine.

★   ★   ★   ★   ★

43

Sir
John Harvey-Jones

☆ ☆ ☆　　　　　　　　　　☆ ☆ ☆

Dogs move in influential circles these days – quite apart from the Queen Mother's favourite corgi, "Ranger", there's Rex Reagan in the White House, and Sir John Harvey-Jones regularly took his dog to the office when he was Chairman of I.C.I..

Sir John served in submarines during the war, and then Naval Intelligence, followed by a distinguished career in industry – you would expect him to have smart pets, and he does – two Alsatians and two Burmese cats.

One of the dogs greatly enjoys green or red peppers, and all types of fruit and vegetables. The only ones he declines to eat are celery and lettuce.

One of the cats, Di-Di, enjoys all types of dog food, and cheese, crisps, salted nuts, curry and cake-icing – right through to sellotape and plastic bags.

Quite a challenge!

In view of his Russian connections and to give an excuse for buying red and green peppers, we offer the following recipe for a cool, relaxing meal of a drink with a definite kick. It can combine aperitif and starter.

44

"In Which We Swerve" – A Russian Gazpacho

4 medium onions
3 cloves garlic (crushed)
4fl.oz/100ml olive oil
2lb/1 kilo tomatoes (skinned and chopped)
2 cucumbers (peeled and chopped)
3fl.oz/75ml red wine vinegar
16fl.oz/500ml water
2 green peppers (chopped and seeded)
2 red peppers (chopped and seeded)
1oz/30g capers (washed and drained)
1 teaspoon celery salt
1 teaspoon Tabasco
juice of 1 lemon
1 teaspoon Worcester sauce
Vodka

- Cook the onions and garlic in the oil gently for about 5 minutes. Add the tomatoes, cucumbers, peppers, water and vinegar. Bring to the boil and simmer for half an hour. Puree the mixture. Add the Tabasco, lemon juice and Worcester sauce, and the salt to taste. Chill for several hours, preferably overnight. This makes lots!
- To serve: (from a large glass or earthenware jug) put generous amounts of ice into each glass. Add a suitable measure of Vodka and top up with "gazpacho", leaving room to stir. Serve with black olives, peanuts and croutons.

★　★　★　★　★

A. L. Rowse

We particularly wanted a good cross-section of contributors to this book, and we were thrilled to have this lovely story of "Peter" from the famous writer and historian, A.L. Rowse.

As he is very much a Cornishman, we thought we would include a recipe for what we understand to be a real Cornish Pasty, according to our Piskie Pals! You can spice it up, but it won't then be the real thing. Certainly some of the articles sold to tourists these days would be more suitable for dry stone walling.

"Feeding My Cats" – by A.L. Rowse

I have nothing very special to say about the feeding of cats. Brought up as I was in a working class home in Cornwall, our family cats had to make do with bread-and-milk, and the scraps that came from the table, left over from meals. They were not spoiled, like the cat of an Australian fan of mine that would eat nothing but salmon. I used to pretend to be shocked, and wonder why it wasn't smoked salmon – which I wouldn't afford for myself!

When I set up my own house I had a cat whom I made a pet of, and he was really something special. I wrote a poem about him, "Peter the White Cat of Trenarren", which is in Philip Larkin's *Oxford Book of Modern Verse,* and I have written his biography, with some others, in *A Quartet of Cornish Cats.*

It is much more difficult to write the biography of an animal than of a person, of a cat than of a queen; for, in the latter case, you have the form and structure given you, the events of her reign, etc.. But I thought that if Virginia Woolf could write the life of Mrs Browning's dog "Flush", then I could write the life of Peter, and I did.

Cats like to have rather grand names. I knew a cat at Oxford who was called Mr Wellington Koo. I have forgotten who that celebrity of the time was, but I have not forgotten the cat. Then a medievalist historian friend of mine called his cats after celebrities of the Middle Ages. Bogo de Clare – Bogo, for short – was a pluralist cleric; Jasper, who had beautiful jade-green eyes, was called after Jasper Tudor, uncle of Henry VII.

My cat was descended from a famous white cat at Bareppa (beau Repaire) near Falmouth, that had belonged to the daughters of John Sterling, friend of Carlyle, who wrote his biography. Peter was given to me by Violet Holdsworth, daughter of the famous historian, Thomas Hodgkin. Hence the names: Peter Rowse Holdsworth Bareppa Trenarren. Peter, for short; sometimes:

Peter Rowse
Caught a mouse
or Peter Rowse
Lives in this house, etc.

He did indeed live with me, and shared my life for sixteen years. Everybody thought he was 'spoiled'; but of course he wasn't. It was Peter who used to spoil me.

Dogs have an endearing habit of bringing a present to someone they know and approve of. Friends of mine had a splendid dog, Apollo; when I came to the door he always brought me a present, usually his master's slipper.

At Polemear Mine my bedroom was on the ground floor. One morning, my cat Peter popped in through the open window with a mouse he thought I might like for my breakfast.

He used to make a recognisable, different cry when bringing a present. At Trenarren I recognised it from up above, when he appeared on the terrace below with a bird for my breakfast. He soon learned, poor little creature, that these presents were not welcome.

He hadn't any peculiarities regarding his own diet – merely that he preferred water to milk. One very hot summer's day he was sleeping under the greenery in the Library border, when I brought him a saucer of cold water. You should have seen the expression of surprise when he awoke and realised what it was; then the expression of gratification when he drank it, without having to get up from his nest.

When I was away, in Oxford or the U.S.A., he had to live mostly on tinned stuff. He wasn't keen; but Beryl, my housekeeper, used to vary the diet to give him a change, and find out what he disliked least.

When I came home then the good times began, for he shared my food. He had a proper liking, for a Cornish cat, of home-made pasty. Served up piping hot to me, I used to blow on his bits to cool them off. Impatient to begin, he yet seemed to understand the point.

If Beryl came by she would laugh to hear me puffing and blowing. When a piece of pasty was still too hot for him he had a way of pouncing on it, stamping with his paw to cool it: a pretty gesture that cats have.

Animals become accustomed to share with those who care for them. At morning tea in bed Peter would consent to lap up some milk, while I drank the tea – though I have known dogs that would drink tea.

Unexpectedly Peter had a liking for home-made sponge-cake – I think he knew the difference from shop cake. In bed he would snuggle up towards my tea-tray, but never eat his cake off the plate. He always had to drag it off the plate on to the counterpane or carpet, as the case might be, before eating. I have never understood why cats do that: can anyone explain it?

Cornish Pasty

homemade shortcrust pastry made from 8oz/240g flour,
    4oz/120g margarine and lard mixed
salt & pepper
8oz/240g chuck steak
2 medium potatoes
small swede
2 medium onions
(makes 2 pasties)

- Roll out the pastry in two rounds to the size of a side plate. Dice the potato and swede very small and put in the centre of the pastry. Add pepper and salt. Cut the meat into very small pieces and place on top of the vegetables. Add the chopped onion on top. Sprinkle a teaspoonful of flour over the top and season again. Finish with a small knob of butter.
- Damp the edges of the pastry and bring together over the top, crimping the edges. Make a small slit in the top for the steam to escape, and brush with egg and milk. Bake at gas 8 (450°F) for 20 minutes and then at gas 2 (300°F) for a further 40 minutes.

★　★　★　★　★

★ ★ ★ ★ ★ ★ ★ ★

Scrummy II:
MAIN COURSES

★ ★ ★ ★ ★ ★ ★ ★

HEATH

✩ ✩ ☆ **Mary Quant O.B.E.** ☆ ✩ ✩

Mary Quant's influence was very much part of our youth, and we hoped very much that she did keep animals, but we secretly wondered if they might interfere with her stylish image.

She didn't let us down, however, as she has two huge dogs – an Old English sheepdog and a Briard. (Come to think of it, they both have to peer through fringes, rather as Mary did in the 'sixties.) They will only eat Whiskas.

The small Shi-Tzu (another fringed example!) has a penchant for fried rice and other oriental food – preferably Cantonese. The Cantonese are into snake, frogs' legs, turtle and, wait for it – dog! Needless to say, we didn't even look for a recipe containing any of those ingredients. However, the Chinese probably consider that we eat some pretty ghastly things too. What must they think of winkles for instance?

★　★　★　★　★

Quantonese Roast Pork

1lb/500g boneless pork shoulder

For the marinade:
1 tablespoon medium sherry
2 tablespoons dark brown sugar
1^1/$_2$ teaspoon salt
1 tablespoon soy sauce
1 tablespoon Hoisin sauce

For the glaze:
2 teaspoons clear honey
2 teaspoons boiling water
2 teaspoons sesame oil

- Cut the meat into long strips approx 5" x 2". Marinate for at least 2 hours.
- Put the meat on a rack in a roasting tin. Roast in a pre-heated oven gas 7 (425°F) for 20 minutes. Remove from the oven and glaze with the honey syrup while still hot.
- Serve cold, with your favourite Chinese addition.

★　★　★　★　★.

51

Geoff Capes

The world's strongest man, Geoff Capes, has two German Shepherd dogs, "Max" and "Mindy". (Well, did you expect Chihuahuas?!)

They are both very active and strong, and are fed on fresh meat and tripe from the local butcher, mixed with meal. When dog-owners say tripe, they are usually talking about the unboiled stuff (not the white slithery variety), and a lot of people, including vets, swear by it. It is not for the squeamish however, and think twice before popping some into the freezer alongside your home-made ice cream. Let us just say that it is unattractive in appearance and ever-so-slightly malodorous.

"Max" and "Mindy" are fond of scrounging when the family is eating, but scraps are given in moderation.

Obviously, as with Geoff himself, the dogs can handle plenty of red meat and protein, as they have plenty of exercise. I think you would have a hard job persuading Geoff Capes to become a veggie, and we certainly wouldn't want to be the ones to present him with a nut cutlet when he came in after lifting a ten-ton truck with one hand. Similarly, after looking at "Max" and "Mindy", if they like raw meat, then who shall argue?

Beefcapes

3lb/1¹/₂ kilos rump of beef
4 slices streaky bacon
1 chilli pepper (seeded and finely chopped)
2lb/1 kilo onions (sliced)
2lb/1 kilo tomatoes (skinned and sliced)

- Lay the beef in an earthenware casserole and cover with the bacon slices. Season with salt and pepper and sprinkle the chilli over. Cover with onions and then the tomatoes. Cover with a sheet of greaseproof paper and a tight-fitting lid. Simmer in a pre-heated low oven gas 2 (300°F) for about 4 hours.
- No liquid must be added.

★   ★   ★   ★   ★

Left-Over Lift Off

12oz/350g fillet steak or underdone sirlion of beef
1 medium onion (finely chopped)
1oz/30g butter
¹/₂oz/15g flour (well seasoned)
1 teaspoon wine vinegar
4 eggs
Tabasco sauce to taste
1 teaspoon fresh chopped parsley
Gravy to moisten

- Cut the meat up into very small pieces – almost minced. Sprinkle the seasoned flour over. Heat the butter in a shallow pan – preferably one you can serve the dish in. Fry the onion and the meat for about 5 minutes. Add the gravy and cook for a further 10 minutes. Add the Tabasco. Poach the eggs and place on top of the meat. Add the vinegar and the parsley
- Grind black pepper generously all over and serve at once.

★   ★   ★   ★   ★

53

Bill Pertwee

Bill Pertwee has appeared on radio, television, the stage and in films more times than you or I and all our dogs and cats put together have had dinners – let alone hot ones!

In recent years he played the harassed ARP warden in the wonderful "Dad's Army", which is one of the few things that no one minds being repeated again and again.

The following rather scrumptious sounding recipe comes not from Bill, but direct from the dog's mouth, so-to-speak.

Biffa obviously has a very deft touch with the typewriter as he sent this to us and obviously has Bill well organised.

★ ★ ★ ★ ★

Biffa's Casserole

"Biffa. Yes, that's my name. I am a black and white Labrador Retriever, with a bit of Border Collie for good measure.

My favourite food is sausage casserole with spinach and crunched bread crusts (wholemeal of course!).

- First, a pound of sausages are partially cooked in a hot oven for 10 minutes. Then the fat is poured off, and gravy poured round the sausages and put back in the oven for a further 15 minutes with the heat turned down.
- While the oven is on, my master cuts up some nice fresh brown bread crusts and puts them in a baking tin to crisp up, while the sausages are cooking.
- Having made sure that all is well, my master then pops down to the bottom of the garden (where the fairies are) and picks some nice green spinach. After washing under running water, he pops it in a large saucepan for two or three minutes with a knob of low fat margarine.
- After cooking, the casserole is allowed to cool, then placed in my bowl, garnished with the brown bread croutons and decorated with spinach.
- I usually woof the lot in 1 minute flat, then have a good sleep for about half an hour after which I'm ready for walkies."

★　★　★　★　★

☆ ☆ ☆ John Aspinall ☆ ☆ ☆

John Aspinall bought Howletts in the late 'fifties as a home for his family and wild animals. As the years passed the herds and colonies of wild creatures grew to such an extent that he decided to ask the public to help defray the mounting cost of upkeep, and in 1975 permission was granted to open the Zoo Park.

However, the presence of the word "zoo" is emotive, and we should like to quote John Aspinall's own words:

"We openly admit at Howletts that here the needs of the wild animals come first... these fifty odd acres belong to them. These rare and lovely animals are not here for the public interest and amusement, they are not exhibits..... they are here to prosper and to propagate, and eventually to return to the wild places that once belonged to them. One of the special features of Howletts is the extraordinary relationship that has developed over the years between keepers and their charges. We hope that a visit to Howletts will invite you to treat the masterpieces of nature with a greater respect. Respect is the secret ingredient that enables a mere human to cross the threshold into nature's realm. The animals here look at you, not through you or past you. They are residents, not inmates, and claim at least a parity with us."

The magnificent silver-back gorilla. "Djoum", is leader of one of the three families of gorillas at Howletts Zoo Park near Canterbury. Whilst there is no question of these animals being regarded as pets, John Aspinall has established a relationship with Djoum – and indeed other animals in his care – based upon trust, respect and love. Most Sundays he will play with the tigers, and afterwards with the gorillas in the walled garden area. He is probably the only man to play with a fully-grown male silver-back gorilla.

The apes are fed on 120 different kinds of food a year. Many of these are imported fruits and vegetables, but a large number of herbs and leaves come from the gardens and estate at Howletts. The gorillas actually look into their food buckets each evening to see what is on the menu. In the wild apes forage for about three hours in the morning, and three hours after their siesta, until they turn in for the night. For this reason, Djoum's food is scattered during the daylight hours. Djoum's favourite foods are: tomatoes, bananas, roast meat, eggs and mangoes.

56

These are the other things that appear on the years' menu: apples, hawthorn, ilex, maple/sycamore leaves, milk, celery, lettuce, Ribena, cucumber, oranges, grapes, Mazuri Primate Diet, primate nuts with trace elements and vitamins, sweet corn, kale, leeks, peaches, radishes, capsicum, chicory, plums, fennel, okra, sugar cane, sweet potatoes, broad beans, convulvulus, peas, pears, cabbage, grapefruit, meat, dates, prunes, sultanas, onions, parsnips, pineapples, potatoes, watercress, peanuts, lemons, turnips, eggs, wheat, chocolate, rice, barley, salt, honey, treacle, juniper berries, beer, thistles, chinese leaf, courgettes, brown bread, lychees, pomegranate, uglis, cocoa, brazil nuts, chestnuts, hazelnuts, almonds, marrow, runner beans, walnuts, cherries, grass roots, beech, sweet chestnut, oak leaves and twigs, blackcurrants, celeriac, parsley, rose leaves and stems, salsify, sea kale, sorrel, raspberries, strawberries, asparagus, mint, basil, blackberries, chinese gooseberries, dill, figs, dried figs, dried apricots, tarragon, jams, guava, dry ginger roots, Horlicks and custard apples! Even most "veggies" don't eat this variety in a lifetime – let alone a year!

☆ ☆ ☆ Ronald Reagan ☆ ☆ ☆

The Reagans love to be informal whenever they can, and are great believers in the powers of natural food – especially honey, which our recipe contains.

Nancy Reagan's pencil slimness is attributed partly to her rule of chewing each mouthful 34 times, and she is a great believer in regular exercise. Obviously a dog is a great incentive for walking – one of the healthiest activities – and isn't it rather nice to think that the "First Family" is human enough to include a dog?

The previous canine incumbent of the White House, the black, shaggy "Lucky", unfortunately didn't live up to his name, but then along came "Rex".

Rex, a Cavalier King Charles spaniel, was a present to Mrs Reagan from the President in 1985. At that time he was almost a year old. He currently lives at the White House, and especially enjoys trips to the country at Camp David. During the week, Rex is Nancy's constant and loving companion, and spends most of the day by her side.

Ronald Reagan never seems to mind being teased about his "cowboy" image, and we felt his recipe just has to be steak. It's very simple – Rex can have the offcuts – and you don't even have to cook it!

Rex Reagan's Rare Beefsteak

Approx 1lb fillet steak

For the marinade:

3 shallots (finely sliced)
6 fresh sage leaves (chopped)
1 teaspoon chopped chives
3 cloves garlic (crushed)
3 tablespoons walnut oil
1 teaspoon grated root ginger
1 chilli pepper (deseeded and
    chopped finely)

1 tablespoon Dijon Mustard
1 tablespoon dark soy sauce
2 tablespoons clear honey
10fl.oz/300ml Budweiser beer
salt & black pepper

- Mix and blend all the ingredients well.
- Freeze the steak sufficiently to allow it to be sliced paper thin. Allow it to return to room temperature while you are preparing the marinade. Cover the meat with the mixture. Cover and put on the bottom shelf of the fridge. Leave for 2 days. Remove the slices from the marinade, and serve, arranged on large flat plates, decorated with sprigs of delicate fresh herbs, such as dill. This makes a delicious starter or snack, but the slices must be very thin if it is to be served raw. Alternatively, cut thicker slices, remove from the marinade and grill or barbecue.

Harry Andrews
C.B.E.

From the often very "macho" parts played by Harry Andrews during his long and very successful acting career, you might expect him to have perhaps a mastiff or boxer – but no! His long-time companion is "Chaval", a wire-haired fox terrier, born in Spain – hence the name, which in Spanish means "naughty boy". Sadly, there are far fewer of this wonderful breed around than there used to be. They are loyal and loving, but at the same time are full of fun and mischief.

The outstretched back legs in Harry Andrews photograph of Chaval are a typical terrier pose. He adores carrots, rabbit and "Good Boys"! He even has his own little swimming pool – otherwise he would dunk himself in the pond and come out black and slightly pongo!

★　★　★　★　★

Peanut Rabbit

1 small rabbit
6 spring onions (finely chopped)
2 tablespoons grated carrot
2 cloves garlic (crushed)
1 teaspoon grated root ginger
3 tablespoons crunchy peanut butter
1 teaspoon wine vinegar
1 tablespoon dark soy sauce
1 teaspoon dark brown sugar
1 teaspoon chilli powder
1 tablespoon sesame oil
8oz/225g cooked rice
4oz/115g salted peanuts

- Soak the rabbit (or rabbit pieces) overnight in water with a little vinegar added.
- Rinse and then either boil or bake gently until well cooked. Allow to cool completely, remove the flesh and shred. Reserve enough for four people and give the remainder to the devoted companion, who will now undoubtedly be right by your side, waiting eagerly for a morsel to drop.
- Mix the rice and the salted peanuts, and put into an eathenware serving dish, making a slight well in the centre. Fill with the shredded rabbit.
- Combine all the other ingredients and spoon over the rabbit. Trim with watercress, curly endive or raddichio.

★　★　★　★　★

☆ ☆ ☆ **Vincent Price**  ★ ☆ ☆

We all know Vincent Price as the Prince of Horror Movies – maybe not quite so well known is his expertise in the kitchen, and his dog was a willing guinea-pig. Vincent Price had "a mutt named Joe. He adored anything with curry in it – not too strong. For days he would have a faint odour of curry – better than his own!"

Our own dog also enjoys curry, and is a demi-veggie, so we have included this recipe. You can make it as strong or as mild as you like, and it should be served with plenty of side dishes: coconut, banana, chutneys, and of course poppodums or chapatis.

★ ★ ★ ★ ★

Mutt's Mediterranean Curry

1/2lb/250g small potatoes (peeled and halved)
1lb/500g aubergines
1lb/500g courgettes
1lb/500g red & green peppers
1lb/500g onions
5fl.oz/150ml olive oil
1lb/500g tomatoes (tinned or fresh)
1 small tin tomato puree
2 teaspoons basil (more if using fresh)
6 cloves garlic (crushed)
2 teaspoons hot curry paste (or according to taste)
1 teaspoon garam marsala

- Wipe the courgettes and slice thickly. Cut the aubergines in four, lengthwise, and slice thickly. Seed the peppers and cut into strips. Peel and slice the onions. Skin and roughly chop the tomatoes.
- Heat the oil in a thick, heavy saucepan or casserole and add the onions, garlic and aubergines. When the onions have softened and the aubergines have absorbed plenty of oil, add the curry paste, garam marsala and basil. Add all the other ingredients and stir well. Don't be afraid to add more oil if you think it is necessary. Cover tightly and cook in a pre-heated oven gas 3 (300°F) for at least an hour.

✩ ✩ ✩ **Sir Geoffrey Howe** ✩ ✩ ✩

We are honoured to include here "The Budget Howe Story", together with a delightful photograph of Budget as a puppy, with Sir Geoffrey's Budget Box.

Budget's favourite food is rabbit. He prefers to have them caught for him, as his time is taken up with weightier matters, as the picture shows.

No-one who has ever owned a Jack Russell ever forgets the experience – our own have enjoyed a variety of foods, including salted pistachio nuts, cold moussaka, Ready-Brek, and almost all forms of live prey, especially uniformed.

Most Jack Russells are to rabbits what Herod was to Moses. Once your beloved pet has rid society of another of these appealing little bundles, it is up to you to present it to him in appetising form. Unlike most of his other prey, this is one delicacy that you can share. We suggest that you make your "Budget Burgers" in the smallest rolls possible – brown or white – and they are ideal for an informal outdoor drinks party, or barbecue.

★　★　★　★　★

From: The Rt. Hon. Sir Geoffrey Howe, QC MP

HOUSE OF COMMONS
LONDON SW1 OAA

BUDGET HOWE STORY

Budget is the second Jack Russell which "We" (the family) have owned. We acquired the first as a "reward" to our eldest daughter, Caroline, for canvassing for me in the campaign (at Bebington) which led to my first election in Parliament in 1964. He was christened Quintin Dogg, because we then lived in Quintin Hogg's constituency, St. Marylebone. He was a profoundly schizophrenic and bad tempered dog, so that our daughter's enthusiasm for him was short lived — and defacto care and control passed to my wife.

When Quintin died, there was a brief (and thankful) hiatus in our dog ownership. But the gap in our family became obtrusive and we decided to risk another Jack Russell, the son of a bitch which belonged to the Devon farming parents of our younger daughter's fiancé. His totally equable temperament is in complete contrast to that of his predecessor.

The name "Budget" was an inspiration of Katherine Whitehorn's — and entirely apt, since Budget was acquired in the Autumn of 1979, six months after we had moved into 11 Downing Street. He is the only dog, so far as I know, whose picture has appeared (together with mine) on the cover of "The Economist" along with the headline (about my 1980 Budget),"Dog Days Budget".

My wife walks Budget at about 7.45 every morning in St. James's Park. He is a most accomplished footballer, to such an extent that several passers-by — on mornings after England have done badly at soccer — have suggested that he and ten of his kind could well replace the entire national team.

64

Budget Burgers

1lb/500g rabbit meat
2 slices of streaky bacon
3 tablespoons fresh chopped parsley
2 shallots
2 cloves of garlic (crushed)
1/2 teaspoon dried sage
1/2 teaspoon dried marjoram
1/2 teaspoon dried thyme
salt and black pepper

- Mince the ingredients, or use a processor, adding a little water to bind. Divide into portions, according to the size of the burgers. (If you can find, or are clever enough to make tiny poppy-seed rolls, these will be ideal for weeny little burgers.)
- Dredge the little nuggets of bunny with flour and barbecue or fry them.
- Serve with dishes of sliced raw onions or shallots, sliced tomato, and a variety of interesting mustards.

★　★　★　★　★

Ken Dodd
O.B.E.

Ken Dodd, still one of our funniest comedians and a pantomime star, says that each of his dogs has had its own particular taste in food.

The last dog would start to dribble at the sight of a Kit Kat label.

The present dog, a poodle named "Doodle", likes a fish, cheese and potato pie, and green veg – and also rice pudding – stirred with the tickling stick!

The Laird of Knotty Ash makes the point that Doodle does not have these dishes specially cooked for him, but the family have been amazed at the relish with which he has tucked into left-overs.

Here's our version of a very tasty fishy pie – for Doodle's sake we hope there are a few remains!

★　★　★　★　★

Doodle Pie

2lb/1 kilo rock fish or coley
1 teaspoon basil
1pt/500ml milk
1 tablespoon olive oil
2oz/60g butter
2oz/60g flour
1 large onion (finely sliced)
2 cloves garlic (crushed)
4oz/125g button mushrooms (cleaned and halved)
1lb/500g tomatoes (skinned and chopped)
1 tablespoon tomato puree
2oz/55g Parmesan cheese (grated)
2oz/55g cheddar cheese (grated)
black pepper
Bay leaf
Choux pastry (most basic cookbooks will have a good recipe, or see
    page 41)

- Skin and bone the fish – properly please, especially if Doodle is getting the left-overs. If you have never experienced a fish bone in the throat, borrow a video of "The Godfather", and watch for the garotting bit.
- Put the fish into a heavy saucepan, add the pepper and basil, pop in the bay leaf and cover with milk. Bring to the boil and simmer very gently until the fish is flaking. Drain the fish and keep the liquor.
- Heat the oil and add the onion and garlic. When they are soft, add the tomatoes, tomato puree and mushrooms. Flake the fish into a deep, square gratin dish – another check for bones please! Cover with the tomato mixture.
- Make a cheese sauce with the butter, flour, two cheeses and the fish liquor, and pour this over the fish and the vegetables.
- Using a wide, patterned nozzle, pipe the choux pastry generously around the edge of the dish. Bake in a pre-heated oven at gas 6 (400°F) or until the pastry is crunchy and golden. A little extra Parmesan can be sprinkled over the top towards the end of the cooking.

★　★　★　★　★

☆ ☆ ☆   ☆ ☆ ☆

Quite unlike some of the dotty characters she played, the late Irene Handl was an actress of genius. She also produced a brilliant novel, *The Sioux*, recently republished; but one of her most endearing characters was in a sketch she wrote, and which she performed with Peter Sellers, when, as the widow of Tufnell she says, with that unmistakable voice (that Noel Coward called "an ineffable veneer of refinement superimposed on basic cockney") "... do you know what he used to call me? "Squidgy". He said: "Squidgy, buy yourself a blue nightie – make your eyes look like stars!".

This happens to be a favourite of Beryl Reid's too, and she named one of her ginger cats "Tufnell", after this great lover!

Chihuahuas may be the smallest of dogs, but they don't know it. They are extremely intelligent, brave and fun to be with, and are certainly not the wimps some people take them to be. We had one who regularly went to the cinema quite unnoticed, until one day he sat up and yawned noisily in the middle of "A Fistful of Dollars". No comment.

Irene Handl sent us this lovely photograph and was quite specific about the feeding of these tiny tums, so we repeat her instructions verbatim.

★   ★   ★   ★   ★

Irene Handl's Recipe For A Healthy Chihuahua:

- "These two little "chis" were my little pals for many years. Beulah was 18 when she died. They were extremely carefully fed, both as to quality and quantity. NO TINS.
- A puddspoonful of porridge (1/2 water, 1/2 milk) for breakfast. Lunch and supper: Very finely cut up, not minced, lean skirt of beef, pan fried (i.e. cooked in a hot, dry frying pan, high, to seal it and then slowly till tender) with a lid on to draw the juice. Add a tiny piece of cooked carrot or cauliflower. 2oz each of this mixture for both meals.
- The treats were occasional "bonne bouches" of custard, boiled sweets, fish, chicken or most popular, a tiny taste of steak and kidney pudding!

★   ★   ★   ★   ★

69

☆ ☆ ☆ Barbara Cartland ☆ ☆ ☆

"I have two dogs. One is a black Labrador which was given to me by Earl Mountbatten of Burma, the Christmas before he was assassinated. He is an excellent gun-dog and is also very good with children.

Like all Labradors, he is greedy, and enjoys all food. He particularly enjoys having in the morning a little of the Bran Crunch, which I always eat myself.

Duke also has D.L.P.A. which is a preventative, as it helps with his rheumatism. It is not a pain-killer, but it strengthens one's own resistance to pain and there are no side effects whatever. I myself have taken it for over a year.

Unfortunately my white Pekingese Twi-Twi, who was the only dog in Madame Tussauds, had to be put to sleep when he was 105 (that is, fifteen), because he went blind. The white Pekingese that I have now was christened Chiang-Mai, and is called Mai-Mai. He is very particular about his food and usually has chicken, but he also enjoys asparagus when I have it.

Both dogs have vitamins in their food. Selenium which prevents cancer, is a healer and keeps them young. Vitamin E which is good for circulation and is what I call "The Life Vitamin". They wait patiently every morning for a tablet of Dessicated Liver, which keeps them active and healthy."

Recipe from Barbara Cartland and her chef Nigel Gordon:

★　★　★　★　★

Luscious Liver

Ingredients:

1/2 pound of liver
Flour
Oil
Vitamin E
Selenium

Method:

- Cut the liver into thin pieces, lightly roll in flour and fry in a little oil for a few minutes. Cool, and then mince the liver.
- Add the Selenium by crushing it and sprinkling it over the liver. Cut the top of the capsule of Vitamin E, and squeeze the oil over the liver.
- Mix it well and serve.

★　★　★　★　★

Dudley Moore

"Curiously, I acquired a dog, a Samoyed – whom we named Minka. She has a predilection for human food to an extent that I have never known in man or beast before! She seems to eat anything – plastic flowerpots, snow peas, fish, strawberries, oranges! In fact, anything that she can get into her ever-open and welcoming mouth. Anything that falls out of the fridge is doomed to her ravenous jaws. I'm amazed that we still have a sofa.

I'm told that Samoyeds do a lot of moaning and groaning which is rather disappointing since I thought we had the only moaning and groaning Samoyed in the world. She makes a strange noise which is halfway between frustration and encouragement. Sitting watching the food from the side of the table and beckoning us with little movements with her head, accompanied by a sort of anticipatory growl – not at all fierce but just enough to assert her presence."

It sounds as though Minka could run the gamut from the worst school dinners to Nouvelle Cuisine, and still beg for more! We thought that this delicious, tangy, garlicky stew might keep her quiet for a while. We serve it with baked potatoes and granary bread for dunking, and the animals enjoy these additions too. The herbs and garlic are wonderful for them, and for cats or tiny dogs you can mince it all up in the processor and freeze in handy-sized portions.

★ ★ ★ ★ ★

"Anything Goes"
(or "Minka's Theme" – a Stew for All Seasons)

1 fresh chicken (or individual legs/drumsticks)
4oz/115g mixture of split peas, lentils and pearl barley
8oz/225g carrots (washed, not peeled and cut into strips)
8oz/225g onions (roughly chopped)
1 large potato (peeled and cut into large chunks)
8 cloves garlic (peeled, left whole)
1 teaspoon basil
1 teaspoon tarragon
chicken stock
pepper

- Soak the lentil mix for several hours or overnight. Drain and rinse.
- Bone and joint the chicken or chicken pieces. (We can hear you whining, but it's really very easy with a good, sharp knife – you don't have to be a brain surgeon – and it eliminates any risk to the animals.)
- Hang on to your giblets and simmer them with the carcass to make stock; you can use a stock cube if you prefer. Brown the chicken pieces quickly in oil or dripping.
- Remove from the pan. Fry the onion and carrot until almost burning and then transfer them to an earthenware casserole. Put the chicken on top and bury the whole garlic cloves in the meat. Add the potato, lentil mix, herbs and pepper. Cover with stock, a layer of greaseproof paper and a tight-fitting lid, and cook in a pre-heated oven gas 2 (300°F) for about 2 hours.
- Because the chicken is so impregnated with scrummy flavours you can leave it to go cold and serve the breast meat, thinly sliced – perhaps inter-leaved with sections of avocado, or nectarine, and served with a crisp, green salad.
- This leaves the rest of the meat, skin and all the veggies for the animals, and everyone is happy!

★ ★ ★ ★ ★

David and Elizabeth Emanuel

David and Elizabeth — the royal wedding dress designers — are a refreshingly young and stimulating couple. They even found the time to design a made-to-measure cashmere donkey blanket, modelled by the Emanuels' own adopted donkey, "The Wicked Lady" — named after one of their clothes collections. They opened a "therapy unit" at The Lockwood Donkey Sanctuary near Guildford, which rescues many ill-treated and abandoned animals.

Their love of animals continues at home where "Poser", a grey, long-haired cat has a passion for fish food (not the first we have heard of), and "Polo", a white, long-haired cat adores spaghetti Bolognese. Liz suggests a special cat recipe could be spaghetti, either with a fresh fish sauce, or a more meaty sauce, made with Kit-e-Kat! Polo also likes eating flowers, sausages, bacon and eggs!

Pasta is very popular, it appears, with many of the animals we have come across in the course of writing this book. As the different shapes and sizes are often interchangeable we have taken the liberty of suggesting a dish with macaroni, but there are lots of alternatives — pasta-loving cats would probably adore vermicelli, which they could play with, like a ball of wool, before, or even during, eating!

Macaroni and Vegetable Casserole

2lb/1 kilo aubergines
2 cloves garlic (crushed)
1lb/500g tomatoes (skinned & chopped)
8oz/250g cooked sliced leeks
8oz/250g cooked cauliflower
3oz/85g shelled fresh peas
12oz/300g macaroni
2 tablespoons fresh chopped parsley
1 tablespoon fresh chopped basil
4oz/100g of your favourite hard cheese
2oz/55g parmesan cheese
1 teaspoon cumin powder
2oz/55g chopped walnuts
olive oil
black pepper and salt

- Wipe the aubergines and remove the stalks. Cut into fairly thin slices and spread on a baking tray. Pour over a generous amount of olive oil, salt, pepper and garlic. Allow to stand for 30 minutes.
- Mix the leeks, cauliflower, peas, tomatoes and cumin. Cook the macaroni in boiling water, to which a drop of oil has been added, simmering for about 10 minutes. Drain well, and stir into the tomato mixture, adding the parsley and basil.
- Pre-heat the oven to gas 6 (400°F). Line the bottom and sides of a large oblong casserole with the aubergine. Fill with the macaroni mixture. Cover the top with the remaining aubergine and sprinkle with a little more olive oil and the parmesan. Bake in the centre of the oven for about 30 minutes, taking care that the parmesan does not burn. We have suggested this recipe, using macaroni, which is sometimes neglected these days, in favour of the trendier forms of pasta. You can also substitute cooked fish for the leeks and cauliflower, or even beef to make it more "Bolognesey".

★   ★   ★   ★   ★

Sue Lawley

It is not just good looks that have won Sue Lawley the title of "Newscaster of the Year". Although she still reads the news, she is a formidable political interviewer – the iron fist in the velvet glove is her approach. Many viewers look forward to Robin Day's hols, if Sue is in the chair for "Question Time".

Not content with that, she has stood in for Terry Wogan on his chat show with great success. He may have the world's most touchable knees, but overall she definitely has better legs!

Sue Lawley's golden retriever, "Cleo", adores Sunday lunch – "the works" – vegetables and all. She is apparently much better than the children at eating up her greens, so obviously she will not be spotty and prey to hideous diseases that we were always threatened with "if you don't eat all your stalks". The only thing Cleo does draw the line at is horseradish sauce, so we hope she won't mind the mustard we have added to the Yorkshire pud.

We have found that a great many dogs enjoy a "Sunday lunch", and their owners get great fun from giving this once-a-week treat. So why not?! It's often quite possible to feed a dog well on what would otherwise be thrown away.

It is very difficult to improve upon the traditional Sunday lunch, and everyone has his/her own favourite way of cooking and serving this most British of meals. There are probably a million different ways of cooking roast potatoes for a start! Here's a way of cooking the Yorkshire pudding that not only adds to the flavour, but saves on the washing up too!

- To your normal Yorkshire pudding batter add a teaspoon of English mustard. 20 minutes before the beef is cooked, take it from the roasting tin and pour the batter immediately into the fat and juice. Put a rack over the tin (leaving enough space to allow the pudding to rise) and put the beef on to the rack. Let the meat cook for 20 minutes longer and then remove it, allowing the pudding a further 10 minutes, or until well-risen and brown.

As an alternative "doggy-bake", make a little extra batter and keep in the fridge. After the meal, chop up any left overs into bite-sized pieces and put into a roasting tin with some dripping or fat, and put into a hot oven. When the fat is smoking, pour in the batter and bake until risen and brown. Allow to cool, chop up and feed to doggie, with a little gravy if you can spare it.

★ ★ ★ ★ ★

Illustration by courtesy of Alexander Gallery Publications Ltd. Bristol. Publishers of Beryl Cook limited editions.

Beryl Cook's hilarious paintings cover a wide range of subjects, and her "naughty-but-nice" style is unique. She has two dogs and two cats, all with a passion for chocolate. (Could it be that the owners are a little partial themselves?)

Beryl and her husband recall "Cedric", a ginger cat, now in heaven (and he doesn't deserve to be!) who adored spaghetti Bolognese. So much so that he would get up on to John's shoulder and with his paw drag the fork away from John's mouth into his own. Cedric is immortalised, gazing at a lobster in Beryl Cook's painting called "Four Hungry Cats".

We thought we would give a recipe for an alternative to Bolognese sauce – you can use any form of pasta of course, but cats probably enjoy the string-like quality of spaghetti!

★   ★   ★   ★   ★

Herb and Walnut Sauce for Spaghetti

4oz/125g chopped fresh herbs: parsley, basil, coriander – anything
    you like, with soft leaves.
2 cloves garlic (crushed)
1 teaspoon chopped chives
2 hard boiled egg yolks
1oz/25g chopped walnuts
1oz/30g soft butter or margarine
pinch of salt
4fl.oz/100ml olive oil
1oz/30g grated Parmesan
1 teaspoon ground paprika

- Process all the ingredients except the olive oil and the cheese. Very gradually, add the oil, while the processer is still going. Finally, stir in the cheese, and fold the sauce into the hot spaghetti. You could, of course, substitute walnut oil for the olive oil.

★   ★   ★   ★   ★

☆ ☆ ☆ **Eamonn Andrews** ☆ ☆ ☆
C.B.E.

We were very saddened by the death of Eamonn Andrews last year. Eamonn is an institution – his gentle authority has made him one of the best-loved television personalities of several decades, and he leaves a sad gap that will never be filled. His reply to us was typically generous and thoughtful.

"We have two labradors, a Jack Russell, and "a black feline moody creature". We long ago stopped giving them cans of pet food, since one of the dogs suffered from a skin rash, and was cured almost instantly by a return to scraps, with perhaps the addition of a couple of pounds of mince a week. We give them all a little breakfast of milk and cereal, otherwise just one main meal, and a spoonful of oil. They all sing in chorus afterwards. If the cat is fed tinned food by mistake it goes a little mad, in an ecstatic kind of way that wouldn't be good for it too often!"

While we don't suggest that you regularly feed your dogs on this rather expensive dish, the name was obviously irresistible, although purists will be horrified at such elaborate additions to the noble fish. If you are lucky enough to live with a labrador, you will already know how closely food must be guarded. Despite the innocent look of that puppy in the Kleenex advertisement, this breed is usually greedy and non too discerning, and will think nothing of scoffing the entire salmon that you have lovingly slaved over. If you have cleaned the fish yourself you could make a very interesting fishy stew for your pets from the head, tail and innards, a little of the broth and the skin chopped up. Add a few potatoes and carrots, but *please remove the bones carefully.*

★ ★ ★ ★ ★

Salmon Labrador (with olive sauce)

1 piece of salmon (about 4lbs/2 kilos)
8oz/250g crab meat
2 tablespoons mayonnaise
1 tablespoon white wine vinegar
1 teaspoon Worcester sauce

6 green olives (chopped)
grated rind of 1 lemon
1 teaspoon chopped fresh parsley
salt and pepper

- Cucumber slices for garnish. Lemon wedges and watercress for decoration.
- Bring to the boil a large pan of water (enough to easily cover the fish), containing a shallot, six black peppercorns, a bay leaf and a pinch of salt.
- Put the salmon in gently and bring just to boiling point again. Allow to bubble very gently for 5 minutes. Turn off the heat and allow the salmon to cool completely in the juice. When cold, remove from the pan (and don't be afraid to plunge your hands in for this delicate job). Remove the skin, bone completely, cover and chill.
- Mix all the other ingredients, add salt and pepper to taste, and stuff into the place where the fish's innards used to be. Decorate the fish with very thin slices of cucumber. Slice generously to serve.

★   ★   ★   ★   ★

Olive Sauce

4 tomatoes (skinned and chopped)
12 black olives (stoned and chopped)
12 green olives (stoned and chopped)
2 hard boiled eggs (chopped)
2oz/55g butter
1 teaspoon paprika
juice of 1 lemon
salt and pepper

- Melt the butter and add the tomatoes. When these are softened, add the rest of the ingredients, stirring gently. Serve warm, with the chilled salmon, but not poured over it.

☆ ☆ ☆ # Clive Brittain ☆ ☆ ☆

When Brough Scott gave up being a National Hunt jockey, he started what has become a very successful, award-winning career in journalism. He is now a familiar face on Channel Four, writing entertainingly and with great knowledge on all aspects of the racing world. He kindly put us in touch with the trainer, Clive Brittain, who told us that both Jupiter Island and Bold Arrangement consume a fair quantity of Guinness and eggs, mixed with their daily feed. Horses in general, and racehorses in particular, have delicate digestions, and incorrect feeding can prove swiftly fatal.

The Queen Mother's famous 'chaser' "Special Cargo" is fed on goats milk – our own pony would drink milk instead of water, given the chance, but has a strange passion for the discarded shells of smoked prawns.

We have devised a hearty stew, containing a good slosh of stout, and what with this and other ingredients, the going should certainly be good! In fact you may need a swift turn of foot to avoid being caught out on the gallops!

★ ★ ★ ★ ★

Beef Casserole With Prunes

2lb/1kg lean neck of beef (cut into 1inch chunks)
1lb/1kg onions (thinly sliced)
4 tablespoons olive oil
3 cloves garlic (crushed)
1 tablespoon tomato puree
1 tablespoon paprika
1 stock cube (dissolved in boiling water)
1/2pt/300ml stout
1/2lb/250g prunes
1/2lb/250g butter beans

Soak the prunes and the beans overnight. Pre-heat the oven to gas 3 (325°F)

- Drain the prunes, reserving the juice. Wash and drain the beans.
- Heat the oil in a deep casserole and seal the meat. Add everything else and stir well until well mixed.
- Cover with a tight-fitting lid and cook for 30 minutes.
- Turn the oven down to mark 2 (300°F) and continue cooking slowly for 2–3 hours or until the meat is flaking. If you think a little more liquid is needed, add some of the prune juice.
- Serve with boiled, mashed or baked potatoes – possibly even some dumplings.

★ ★ ★ ★ ★

☆ ☆ ☆ **Stirling Moss O.B.E.** ☆ ☆ ☆

Although retired from Formula One racing, Stirling Moss still likes life in the fast lane from time to time, and certainly enjoys good food.

He is yet another "Westie" fan, and the one before his present dog, "Caesar", made it to 16 years of age, so this diet is worth looking into.

Mrs Moss had a German Shepherd who enjoyed the odd avocado, and they both had a very strange Jack Russell who liked mixed salads. In fact this is not at all unusual – our dog loves salad, as did his grandfather, with plenty of French dressing. We get the impression that the Moss Jack Russell was altogether strange, as only a J.R. can be!

We include Caesar's own recipe for a long and healthy life, together with a de luxe version.

★ ★ ★ ★ ★

Caesar's Recipe

1oz/30g chicken or white meat   1/2oz/15g hard cheese
1oz/30g green veg   2–3oz/approx 50g dog biscuits

- Mixed together with warm gravy made from white meat bones.

★ ★ ★ ★ ★

Caesar's Grand Prix Recipe

4 small turkey breasts (approx. 6oz/180g each)
8-10 cooked Brussels sprouts (mashed with butter)
4oz/120 grated cheddar or other hard cheese
1 tablespoon chopped fresh tarragon
grated rind of a lemon
2oz/55g chopped pecan nuts
black pepper
12oz/250g ready-made puff pastry
egg (beaten)
4 tablespoons cranberry sauce or jelly

- Make a decent sized pocket in the breasts. Mix together the sprouts, cheese, tarragon, lemon rind and nuts, and season well with black pepper. Divide the mixture into four and carefully stuff each breast.
- Divide the pastry into four and roll out sufficiently to enclose the breasts. Smear a spoonful of the cranberry sauce on top of each breast. Wrap the turkey in the pastry and seal with the egg. Make two slits in the top and decorate with pastry off-cuts. Brush with the beaten egg and put onto a baking tray.
- Put in the fridge and pre-heat the oven to gas 7 (425°F). Bake for 15 minutes and then turn the heat down to gas 4 (350°F) and cook for a further 35 minutes.

This can be accompanied by a creamy tarragon sauce, as follows:

5fl.oz/175ml dry white wine   5fl.oz/150ml double cream
1 tablespoon fresh chopped tarragon   black pepper

- Cook the wine with the tarragon in a small saucepan until reduced to about 2 teaspoons. Add the cream, grind in some pepper and allow to bubble until slightly thickened. Strain.

Michael Barrymore

An extremely popular comedian and quiz show host, Michael Barrymore breeds West Highland White terriers as a hobby. All terriers usually have a sense of humour, and while we are not actually suggesting that Michael practises his jokes on an audience of "Westies", they probably give him a few laughs and help him to unwind.

"Candy"'s favourite meal is a mixture of chicken, rice and scrambled egg – this made us think of kedgeree, which is usually a breakfast dish. With the addition of chicken it could easily be lunch or supper.

This spicy variation is adapted from an Indian book that tells you how to white-wash bungalows, make home-made "Flit" and mend a mackintosh – so be warned!

★ ★ ★ ★ ★

Kedgeree

3oz/85g rice
3oz/85g lentils
2oz/clarified butter
1 onion (sliced)
4oz/115g cooked chicken (flaked)
4oz/115 smoked haddock (cooked & flaked)
1 egg (scrambled)
6 cloves
two sticks cinnamon
3 or 4 cardomums
10 peppercorns
1 teaspoon salt
16fl.oz/500ml water

- Soak the lentils. Wash and drain. Wash and drain the rice. Heat the butter, brown the onion in it and remove. Put in the spices and fry them. Reduce the heat and add the rice and lentils. Heat up again and add the salt and water. Cover and simmer until all the water is absorbed and the grains are tender.
- Remove the cloves and other spices – if you can find them (if not, just remember to tell everyone that they are there!) Gently blend in the chicken, fish, egg and onions. Moisten with a little milk or cream if necessary, and warm gently through before serving.

★　★　★　★　★

☆ ☆ ☆ Robert Hardy C.B.E. ☆ ☆ ☆

In view of the title of our book, we couldn't leave out Robert Hardy, who portrayed Siegfried Farnon so brilliantly in "All Creatures Great and Small". Siegfried was always followed by a pack of dogs of all shapes and sizes, which cannot have been difficult to arrange, as Robert Hardy is a great lover of animals. He has given us the following recipe:

★ ★ ★ ★ ★

Healthy Diet for a Gazehound or Whippet

Two or three cupfuls of organically grown porage oats boiled in water for a minute or so.

Turn off the heat and poach in the still bubbling porage two ounces of diced lamb's liver.

Add, if you have it, wild rabbit, cooked in its own juice without any addition, except water.

Add, from time to time, mashed potato and greens or carrots, which must also have been cooked only in water.

If you can forbear to eat it yourself, serve to the dog in question.

★ ★ ★ ★ ★

Scrummy III: AFTERS

★ ★ ★ ★ ★ ★ ★

★ ★ ★ ★ ★ ★ ★

Terry Wogan

Not for Terry Wogan a perky Irish Terrier, or even a pair of labradors to spread before the hearth at Wogan Towers; instead, a beautiful Weimaraner, called Alliss. These are sort of "designer dogs", in a fetching shade of dove grey, with questioning pale eyes.

"Alliss, rather like her beloved master, is fond of her grub, and will eat anything! We thought they might like to sample the Guinness Loaf? Oh well...... maybe just a half then, if you insist!

★ ★ ★ ★ ★

Guinness Loaf

8oz/225g sultanas
1oz chopped whole blanched almonds
6fl.oz Guinness or other stout
8oz/225g self raising flour
1 beaten egg
4oz/115g soft dark brown sugar

- Soak the fruit overnight in the Guinness. Strain, and keep the liquid. Mix all the ingredients and add the Guinness – a little extra may be needed, which you will have left, won't you? Or did you think that bit left in the bottle was the cook's perk?
- Line the bottom of a 2lb loaf tin with greased greaseproof paper. Spoon in the mixture and bake in a pre-heated oven gas 4 (350°F) for 1 hour or until a metal skewer comes out clean.
- Turn out and allow to cool. Store in foil to keep moist. Slice thinly, spread with butter.

★ ★ ★ ★ ★

Obviously, hard work is the secret of eternal youth – Deborah Kerr changes little, and continues to grace our screens in the true sense of the word.

She now lives in Spain, and has been taken over by her beautiful tortoiseshell cat:

"I am the proud owner of a cat known as Kit-e-Kat (the only name our Spanish maids could pronounce!) or, rather, she is the proud owner of Me!

Kit-e-Kat very much enjoys a mixture of chopped grapes and cheese!

I have a small green watering can for my plants – and one very hot day I noticed Kit-e-Kat standing with one paw inside the watering can. She was telling me very clearly that I had forgotten to fill her water dish that morning. What a cat! She doesn't need to speak!"

Grape Brulee

1lb/450g large grapes (peeled, seeded and drained)
2 tablespoons brandy
3oz/85 dark brown sugar
1/2 pint/10fl.oz whipping cream
2oz/50g cream cheese
1 teaspoon fresh lemon juice

- Cover the base of a china flan dish with the grapes. Pour over the brandy. Soften the cream cheese with the lemon juice. Add the cream and beat until stiff.
- Spread this mixture over the grapes and chill in the freezer until just firm. Sprinkle over the brown sugar and put under a hot grill until the sugar is caramelized and bubbling. Remove and chill.

★　★　★　★　★

☆ ☆ ☆ Catherine Cookson ☆ ☆ ☆
O.B.E.

Animals did not play an important part in the life of the young Catherine Cookson, which she describes with great sensitivity and humour in her autobiography, "Our Kate". And you will find no recipe for gourmet meals in this vivid account of life in the North East between the wars.

Since the war, however, and her hard-won fame and fortune, Catherine Cookson and her husband have had three dogs, spanning the years.

"The first was Bill a Bull Terrier, given capitals, a wonderful dog who loved people, but hated all other dogs; then came Simon, as good a dog as golden Labradors can be. He didn't discriminate, except that he adored oranges, and had a pastime of tearing up teatowels.

Last, Sandy, the poodle, now 13$\frac{1}{2}$ and eating anything, but with a strong penchant for cheese and chocolate". Catherine Cookson has not always enjoyed the best of health although this has never stood in the way of her passion for writing, much to the delight of her millions of readers all over the world. She has taken an interest in diet − writers often have to be rather careful because when you're not just sitting scribbling, you're just sitting thinking about what to scribble, so scoffing is not a very good idea!

★   ★   ★   ★   ★

Sandy's Candy Boxes

1oz/25g castor sugar
1oz/25g flour
1 egg
1 tablespoon water (warm)

For the filling:

5fl.oz/150ml water
5oz/150g packet orange jelly
1 teaspoon fresh orange juice
8oz/225g cream cheese (softened)
10fl.oz/300ml whipping cream
2 tablespoons marmalade (without peel)

For the boxes:

64 After Eight mints (keep chilled)

To decorate:

- Grate long ribbons of orange peel and tie in knots
- Line the base of a 7 inch square cake tin with greased greaseproof paper. Whisk the egg and sugar until pale and frothy. Fold in the flour and water and pour into the prepared tin. Bake in a pre-heated oven gas 6 (400°F) for approximately 10 minutes or until well-risen and golden. Turn out on to a wire rack, peel off paper and leave to cool.
- Heat the water and dissolve the jelly in it. Add the orange juice. Put into the fridge for about 30 minutes or until the mixture is syrupy.
- Beat the cheese and gradually add the jelly, beating all the time. Whip the cream, and fold in two thirds. Pour the mixture into a 7 inch square cake tin lined with greaseproof paper. Chill for about 2 hours, or until set.
- Warm the marmalade slightly, and brush the sponge with it. Turn out the cheese mixture on to the sponge square. Remove the greaseproof paper and neaten up the edges.
- Cut the "cheesecake" into sixteen 1¹/₂ inch squares. Take the After Eights from the fridge and gently press one on each of the 4 sides of the little cakes. Pipe a rosette of cream on top of each little box, and decorate with a knot of orange peel.

★   ★   ★   ★   ★

Dame Daphne du Maurier

The novelist and playwright, Daphne du Maurier, was created a Dame in 1969. Looking at this charming photograph of Dame Daphne and her companions, it is hard to believe that she was a contemporary of Noel Coward and Gertrude Lawrence. She still lives in Cornwall, setting of one of her most famous novels, *Jamaica Inn.*

Although these two West Highland terriers, "Mac" and "Ken", have no particular likings, they look so handsome and healthy we couldn't leave them out. They do enjoy a sweet biscuit each for tea, however, and so we've christened our home-made (and very cheap!) dog biscuits after them.

★　★　★　★　★

McKenbix

- Save left-over pastry, or make some in the normal way. Puff pastry scraps are very good, and the more the pastry has been mauled, the better, as you don't want it to be too light and crumbly. If you have ghastly mistakes, you can always say that you were making dog biscuits. It will help your credibility if you have a dog.
- Add the chosen flavouring, chopped fairly small, and blend well. More mauling, or use the processor and don't worry if you overdo it.
- Man/womanhandle the dough into a long, square-ish sausage and cut into 1/4 inch slices. Place on a baking tray on the floor of the oven, preferably when you are already cooking something fairly slowly. Bake for ages. Even forget. You should end up with some inexpensive, rock-hard little numbers that the dogs will adore.

Suggested flavourings:

walnuts and honey, peanuts, stilton, cheddar, garlic and parsley, tomato puree and basil

★   ★   ★   ★   ★

Mike Yarwood
O.B.E.

Mike has made life very easy for us all by providing a delicious "bird mixture" recipe.

He has had the usual variety of animals over the years – dogs, gerbils, hamsters and a pony, but none has had a peculiar eating habit, unless we count an armchair and curtains!

He is obviously fond of birds, but says that they fly off when he goes into the garden, so a photograph with them was out of the question! Maybe he should add St. Francis to his already incredible range of impersonations?

★ ★ ★ ★ ★

Mike's ingredients are:

Suet	Raisins
Potatoes (boiled or roast)	Rice
Meat bones/Chicken carcass	Over-ripe fruit
Bacon rinds	Black pudding

We suggest baking this lot together when you already have the oven on. Allow to cool and set and put the whole thing, in the tin, out in the garden – well out of the reach of cats. You will have hours of enjoyment and maybe attract a whole new clientel.

Colin Willock

Colin Willock is the producer of the award-winning Anglia Television "Survival" programmes, and is himself a lover of, and expert on, the countryside and the creatures and humans that dwell therein.

He is an amusing raconteur and has written many books, including the hilarious account of his Jack Russell, "Dudley, the Worst Dog in the World". Colin very kindly gave us permission to quote this excerpt from "Landscape with Solitary Figure" (published by Andre Deutsch) and sent this picture of the innocent-looking, handsome, but devastatingly greedy "Drake".

"Drake, a black and white Springer of great character, much of it bad. He performed miracles of gourmandisation at an early age, being particularly partial to butter, which he scoffed by the half pound with the paper still in situ. The children said it was good for his coat. His most remarkable feat took place on an afternoon when my wife was preparing for our twins' birthday party. She had just made forty-two sausage rolls – she remembers the number precisely – and, having removed them from the oven, had put them on the table to give both the rolls and herself a chance to cool off. Neither was able to drop much below boiling point. In the time it took her to walk to the sitting room, light a cigarette, inhale deeply once and return to the kitchen, Drake had moved in. She found him licking the last crumb of the forty-second roll from his chops.

Even she admitted later that he done something unequalled in his own limited field. These sausage rolls were too hot for the human hand, let alone stomach, to touch. As far as I know this feat still stands as a minor world record."

John Francome
M.B.E.

We usually think of champion National Hunt jockey, John Francome, in connection with horses, but John and Miriam Francome do have other animals, including Miriam's unusual collection of rare poultry.

Hazel, the Partridge Cochin, is very keen on breakfast, preferably in the kitchen. She eats most things – bacon rinds, toast and jam, the cat's food, even fried egg, but she has her favourite, which the Francomes have named after her.

Since his retirement from professional riding, John has written several very amusing and informative books, and has even started his own club for racegoers, organising trips to all the major race meetings at home and abroad, a dinner and even an open day at the Francomes' yard in Lambourn.

★　★　★　★　★

Hazel's Delight

4oz/115g seedless grapes
8fl.oz/250ml "Total" Greek strained yoghourt
2oz/50g Grapenuts

- Mix all the ingredients thoroughly.
- This makes quite a quantity of breakfast and even Hazel couldn't eat quite all this – luckily John and Miriam like it themselves.
- Strawberries may be used instead of, or as well as, the grapes.

★　★　★　★　★

☆ ☆ ☆ Young's Brewery ☆ ☆ ☆

This famous brewery has been in Wandsworth since 1675, and the magnificent Shire horses still draw the drays of beer in South London.

The horses have mild ale mixed with their feeds, which includes malt grains from the mash after most of the extract for beer making has been "sparged" out. Most of the horses enjoy a drink of beer and are very fond of peppermints, as is Ram Rod, a Dorset Horn ram, the brewery mascot and trade mark. Ram Rod 4 is the latest in a famous line – Ram Rod 1,2 & 3 all met the Queen on various occasions!

Wandle Steve, the beautiful black gelding in the picture, was presented with a magnificent cake on his 21st birthday, made of horse feed, twenty-one carrots and the word Stevie spelled in sugar lumps. He also had a seven piece band play "Happy Birthday", and the children of Wandsworth ran behind his dray shouting, "He's twenty-one today!" The head horse-keeper explained: "Stevie is our oldest horse. We wanted a special day for him. He knows his round backwards and stops at all the right pubs. Last Friday he even popped into one of them for a drink".

We've used beer in our recipe for a chocolate cake – horses are not averse to the odd nibble of chocolate, though it proved very costly for a certain racehorse whose win was disqualified when his routine dope test proved positive after a stable girl had given him a bite of her Mars bar!

Chocolate Cheers Cake

8oz/225g plain flour
6oz/170g caster sugar
4oz/115g butter (softened)
2 eggs
1 level teaspoon baking powder
1/4 teaspoon bicarbonate of soda
2oz/55g plain dark chocolate
7fl.oz/200ml lager
pinch of salt

For the filling:
4oz/115g butter (softened)
8oz/225g icing sugar
4oz/115g plain dark chocolate
(melted)

- Pre-heat oven to gas 4 (350°F) and grease two 8" cake tins. Sieve together the flour, salt, baking powder and bicarbonate. Melt the chocolate and allow to cool. Cream the butter and sugar until pale and fluffy. Beat the eggs and gradually add to the butter and sugar. Beat in the melted chocolate.
- Add the flour and the lager, bit by bit, and beat well. Divide the mixture between the two tins and bake for 25 minutes. Cool on a rack.
- Whisk the filling ingredients and spread on both halves, sandwich together and spread remaining chocolate cream on top. Decorate with yet more grated chocolate.

Mr and Mrs Louis Freedman

"I have an affinity with animals, whether horses, dogs, cats or even mice. I love God's creatures."

Louis Freedman went into horse ownership for fun, nearly thirty years ago, and he has certainly not only achieved this for himself, but for a great many others who get pleasure from seeing a good horse.

His remarkable son of Mill Reef, Reference Point, has carried the Freedmans' colours home to victory in major races, including The Derby and the St. Ledger, and our recipe reflects the famous yellow with black spots!

The Freedmans live at Cliveden, in Berkshire, with their beautiful Great Dane.

"Elka has always been a fussy eater, but has not been known to refuse a meal which consists of: a handful of Winalot or equivalent, soaked in gravy, and a mixture of tripe, lambs tongue and hearts, which can be enlivened with some snippets of chicken or beef or (great delight) grouse. If, after this, one can produce a little of any pudding with cream, then she is a very happy dog."

The Freedmans' first Great Dane, Esther, very kindly helped open the mail one day, which contained some wedding cake, complete with silver horseshoes that stuck to her mouth and gave the game away.

In spite of their size, Great Danes are not usually greedy eaters and in fact often have to be tempted with tasty morsels. We suggest that Elka would love her own private little omelette – without the rum and blackcurrants, but with plenty of cream.

The Yellow with Black Spots Celebration Omelette

Per person:

1–2 eggs (depending on size and greed)
2oz/55g fresh blackcurrants (topped and tailed)
2 tablespoons soft dark brown sugar
1 tablespoon dark rum
1 tablespoon caster sugar
knob of butter
Masses of whipped cream

- Wash and drain the blackcurrants, reserving a few for decoration. Put the fruit into a saucepan with the brown sugar and cook gently until just softening. Add the rum and keep warm.
- Separate the eggs and whisk yolks and whites until frothy and stiff respectively. Fold together. Melt the butter in an omelette pan and pour in the egg mixture.
- Cook gently, and when the underside has set, put in the fruit mixture. Fold the omelette and turn out at once on to a plate. Sprinkle with the reserved blackcurrants, as evenly as possible. Serve with whipped cream.
- N.B. Please use free-range eggs – firstly the chickens will thank you, and secondly the yolks should be a brighter yellow.

★　★　★　★　★

Elaine Paige

☆ ☆ ☆   ☆ ☆ ☆

Elaine Paige's dog really ought to be called a "West End Terrier", as that is where Elaine has spent so much of her time since her overnight success in "Evita". She also starred in "Hair", and says that she almost became a full-time hippy at one time! Luckily for us, she changed her mind!

Elaine's Westie, "Tugger", is quite a fussy eater. He will only eat fresh food, which Elaine has to cook for him every day. He likes chicken breasts cooked in Oxo, with onions, and then chopped up with greens, grated carrot and a slice of brown bread! The meat can vary, as long as it is tender, lean and tasty!

Elaine says that it's rather like looking after a child because she actually has to cook the meal each day — no tins for Tugger! As a treat he loves chocolate, but only Cadbury's Dairy Milk — he won't touch any other brand! We thought this chocolate drink might provide a treat for them both.

★　★　★　★　★

Chocoholics Nightcap

1 pint/16fl.oz milk
4oz/115g Cadbury's Dairy Milk Chocolate
2oz/50g dark brown sugar
3fl.oz/75ml dark rum
pinch of cinnamon

- Combine all but the rum in a saucepan and heat gently until the sugar dissolves and the chocolate melts. Stir all the time.
- Add the rum and whizz in the blender or processor until frothy. Pour into warm mugs and grate a little chocolate on the top. Sleep well!
- A microwave is brilliant for making drinks like this. Use a larger cup or mug and don't fill it right up; stir halfway through the cooking time. It's still nice to froth it up afterwards, but there's no saucepan to wash up.

★　★　★　★　★

☆ ☆ ☆ **Bernard Cribbins** ☆ ☆ ☆

The dear, departed "Booby" had a passion for crab apples, and when the fruit was ripe, she would sit underneath the tree and wait for falling goodies! She would also "will" you to come out and shake the tree to dislodge the fruit.

Beagles are well-known for the ability to manipulate – they nearly always get what they want, and every time you fall for it, you curse yourself for being so gullible! The beagle of our acquaintance, the appalling, but much-loved "Dicky Neville", probably still haunts the country lanes, cocking his leg on the newly-picked apples in Sheffield Park, and making offers they never could refuse to the ladies of East Sussex, where his progeny still abound.

Obviously "Booby" made a lasting impression upon the Cribbins family, and luckily for us, the same is true in the theatre and cinema, and on television and radio of Bernard Cribbins who pops up regularly and can always bring a smile – anyone owned by a beagle has to have a good sense of humour!

There are not many ways of using crab-apples, but we have found this recipe makes a change from cranberry sauce – delicious with cold meat, especially pork or game.

Pickled Crab Apples

1lb/450g dark brown sugar
16fl.oz/500ml cider vinegar
12fl.oz/350ml water
Grated rind of 1 lemon
Grated rind of 1 orange
cinnamon stick
1 teaspoon ground ginger
1 teaspoon ground allspice
2 cloves
3lbs/1.35 kilos small, evenly-sized crab apples

- Wash the crab apples thoroughly, being careful to leave the stalks on where possible. Bring all the ingredients (except the apples) gently to the boil and simmer for 10–15 minutes. Add the apples. Simmer for a further 10 minutes, or until the apples are just tender.
- Transfer the fruit with a slotted spoon to sterilized pickling jars. Boil the liquid fiercely for about 10 minutes to reduce it, and then pour it over the apples to cover. Seal the jars and store in a cool place.

★　★　★　★　★

☆ ☆ ☆ **Joan Littlewood** ★ ☆ ☆

Joan Littlewood has been a powerful, often controversial force in the theatre. Her "theatre workshop" gave many of today's "names" their first taste of the stage, and her direction of "Oh What a Lovely War!" was highly acclaimed.

She now lives mainly in France, and we are delighted to relate the story of her first encounter with "Tati", who is now her much-loved companion.

★　★　★　★　★

"A Picture Of Tati"
by Joan Littlewood

He picked me up in a little French town which I'd never even heard of till this cold February day. I should have looked at the footnotes to that timetable in the ticket office. The clerk said nothing as he sold me a ticket to Pointe-de-Grave.

I was spending a long week-end with friends who had told me that their home was ideal for quiet work – but by Sunday evening it was more like a parrot-house and none of these bright characters showed signs of leaving on the following morning.

A slow train to the loneliest spot on the map was the only solution...

Someone was tapping on the carriage window. Something told me that the train had been stopped for rather a long time.

"Point-de-Grave?'

He opened the carriage door.

"This is as far as we go, madame... in winter."

A flurry of snow brushed my cheek as I stepped down.

"Where are we?"

"Lesparre".

"And the next train back?"

"Seventeen-ten".

Beyond the mini-station there were bare fields, in the distance grey silhouettes of human habitation against a darkening sky but somewhere there must be a cosy café where I could sit in the corner and scribble.

When I reached the streets, all the shops were closed and shuttered. I'd forgotten the French Monday. I plodded on, the roads were empty – not much chance of a hitch-hike.

'Ah, the "Cafe de la Liberation" and it might even be open. You couldn't tell. It looked like one of those cheerless dumps where immigrant workers sit endlessly over minute coffee cups. It was. All eyes turned on me as I made my way to the counter.

This was no place for random dawdlers. My coffee entitled me to the very shortest stay.

In no time I was back on the freezing street. I could see a tall spire in the distance and decided to take a look at the church, it might even offer a bit of shelter. I was walking fast when I heard a little dog yapping. I looked round, a Pekinese was jumping at an elegantly built dog, three times it's height – elegant but painfully thin and weak.

As I stopped a woman came out of the house opposite and picked up the Pekinese.

I asked her if she knew where the other dog came from.

111

"He's been knocking around here for weeks", she said. "That's all I know" — and went.

The starving dog looked at me. His eyes were the colour of dark honey, his sharp face chocolate brown, his breast white. He wore no collar.

I had no food to give him and tried to tell him so. He followed me as I made for the church and every time I turned, he stopped and gave me his old fashioned look. His legs were so long and slender, flecked with that same chocolate brown. His tail had been docked.

I sat on a bench gazing at Lesparre's bleak Gothic, he sat beside me. I couldn't have entered the church, anyway.

All the doors were locked.....

At the police station they shrugged me off.

"Oh madame! There are so many abandoned dogs..."

I could turn him in, they said.

"And then?"

"He'll be put down".

We left. Back at the same sad café, I pocketed two sugars from the dish. He was waiting for me and scrunched them rapidly.

Now what do I do with you?

I couldn't expect my friends to accept him. They were, in any case, pedigree minded and had a dog of their own — Rajah, a Labrador.

I'd better get back to my writing and forget about stray dogs. The station was the only place open to me and I made my way there, ruminating over the unwritten article. I opened the gate. I turned. Who was there, looking up at me?

Explaining that we had come to a parting of the ways I sadly closed the gate. As I moved towards the shelter of the ticket office a brown and white shape appeared at the furthest end of the platform — almost running and, I swear, smiling.

God knows how he had found another way on to the platform so quickly -

"Give me a dog ticket, first class," I said to the country chap in the booking office.

"A proper chien-de-chasse", he said, "I'd take him for a pointer".

Of course there were no classes on that lumbering old local train when it finally arrived. Tati took his ease across my lap.

All this happened five years ago and now I have a handsome cooky character on my hands. He has developed a slight wave in his glossy coat and even a little feather on the end of his tail.

He is the fastest dog you ever saw — and the funniest. That is why he is called Tati, after Jacques of that ilk. If he thinks I have worked too long, he pinches my writing paper. If he can get into the bathroom he will pinch any intimate article of underclothing to make me chase him. After our early morning walk he shares my two rounds of French bread. I think he grew up in a poor home and was fed on dry bread. He still has a taste for it, demands it. His main meal is a bowl of rice

112

or pasta mixed with morsels of meat. He won't eat vegetables. He is no gourmand, never devours his food as other dogs do and best of all he likes to wait for tasty bits from my plate, chicken above all, like all dogs.

When I come to England he stays with my friend, Jeannine, and I bring him back those all-shapes and colours dog biscuits, which he loves.

He is a character with many interests. He calls on friends, investigates hedgehogs, leaps after birds but never catches them, digs endlessly by the stream but never finds anything.

He is a comedian.

★ ★ ★ ★ ★

Pain Perdu

Tati does not pretend to be a gourmet – he hates vegetables and he knows what it is to be hungry. So here is a little nourishing dish, which can be breakfast lunch or supper, served with sausage, bacon – maybe jam. Even alone.

4 slices white bread (medium cut)
1/4 pt/150ml milk
1oz/25g butter
2 large eggs

- Lightly beat the eggs. Add the milk. Dip each slice of bread in the mixture, coating both sides. Heat the butter until it is just about to colour. Fry the bread on both sides until golden brown. Eat immediately – unless you are a dog, in which case allow it to cool down slightly!

★ ★ ★ ★ ★

No one deserves his success more than Steve Davis, although he would be the first to admit that he couldn't have done it without the encouragement and support of his parents. It is Steve's mum, Jean Davis, whom we have to thank for this recipe for Carrot Cake, which she bakes for the family and the two Rottweilers, "Spot" and "Plain". (She hopes you'll recognise Steve in the middle of the photo!) Spot is on the left and Plain on the right. The dogs have become very partial to carrot cake and come running whenever they smell it!

★　★　★　★　★

Carrot Cake

8oz/225g margarine (polyunsaturated)
8oz/225g light soft brown sugar
5oz/140g self-raising flour
5oz/140g self raising wholemeal flour
4 eggs (lightly beaten)
grated rind and juice of 1 orange
4oz/115g ground almonds
8oz/225g English carrots (washed & grated, but not peeled)

- Cream together the margarine and sugar. Work in the eggs, and then fold in the flour. Finally, fold in the almonds, carrots and orange. Put the mixture into a greased and base-lined 8 inch cake tin and level the surface. Bake at gas 4 (350°F) for $1^1/_2$ hours until golden brown. Turn out and cool on a wire rack.
- The Davis Family, including Spot and Plain, eat it just like this, but you can sprinkle with sieved icing sugar, or use a lemon water icing, or even cream cheese icing.

114

Joan Rivers ☆ ☆ ☆

Joan Rivers almost defies description – she has been called "the world's funniest lady". Despite her risque and brittle humour, and at the risk of shattering an illusion, she's much more of a "softie" than she'd have us believe.

Joan has three dogs – German shepherds, Tiger and Shasta, and a Lhasa Apso named Sparky. They live on things that Joan thinks others would die from – not true! Melon crops up all the time, with dogs, cats, sheep and horses. In the Rivers' household they go for canteloup, chocolate cake, cold pasta, and soufflées. Who eats whose left-overs?!

Joan's dogs would love charentais melon, with it's rather Yves St Laurent aroma, which we like to fill with cottage cheese, and strips of smoked salmon. The chocolate pudding is a friend's recipe, with the name changed to avoid contravening the Race Relations Act and upsetting Mrs Whitehouse.

Shasta and Tiger please note: we did have a recipe for "Alsatian Cheesecake", but we thought it would be in rather poor taste!

★   ★   ★   ★   ★

Hoddy Boddy Pudding

5oz/140g butter
5oz/140g caster sugar
5oz/140g Cadbury's drinking chocolate
5oz/140g ground almonds
4 eggs (separated)

- Cream the butter and the sugar. Add the beaten yolks of the eggs. Add the ground almonds and chocolate and mix well. Beat the egg whites until stiff, and fold into the mixture. Put into a pudding basin and cover. Steam for 2 hours. Serve with thick cream.

★   ★   ★   ★   ★

Robin and Louella Hanbury-Tenison

While on holiday in the South of France, the explorer, Robin Hanbury-Tenison, and his wife Louella, saw the beautiful white horses of The Camargue. (They were lucky – all we saw were the extremely unattractive black mosquitoes of The Camargue!) They needed two horses to round up cattle and sheep on their farm on Bodmin Moor, so they decided to ride the 1200 miles from France to Cornwall.

Tiki and Thibert were the first Camargue horses to come to Britain. They are both mad about sugar and apples, and on the long trek they were given windfalls, to augment the buckets of cakes carried in the escort cars. Camargue horses are designed to live rough, and hate being indoors — a few days in racehorse luxury would probably kill them! Tiki and Thibert are now much-loved members of the Hanbury-Tenison team — brilliant at rounding up the cattle, and a constant reminder of a great adventure (recounted in a book called *White Horses Over France*).

We like to serve sorbet in the hollowed out shells of whatever fruit has been used for the flavour — rather tricky when it comes to blackcurrants! Apples are ideal for this, and you can keep the shells in the freezer for months. Sometimes guests will want to eat the frozen shells as well as the contents, but in our case — and especially with pineapples — we save them for our prawn-eating pony, who loves these slightly icey treats from time to time!

★   ★   ★   ★   ★

Cider Sorbet

10oz/285g granulated sugar
18fl.oz/575ml strong cider
1 teaspoon lemon juice
1 large egg white
pinch of cream of tartar
pinch of salt
8fl.oz/250ml water

- Put the sugar and water into a saucepan, and bring to the boil. Stir until the sugar dissolves, and then allow to cool. Bring the cider to the boil and simmer for 5 minutes. Allow to cool.
- Combine the cider with 9fl.oz/280ml of the syrup, and the lemon juice, in a bowl over ice, and stir until it is chilled. Freeze for about an hour, until not quite frozen.
- Beat the egg white with the salt. Add the cream of tartar and continue beating until stiff. Fold into the cider mixture and freeze.
- Serve in frozen scooped out apples.

★   ★   ★   ★   ★

117

✩ ✩ ✩ **Maureen Lipman** ✩ ✩ ✩

Maureen Lipman's wonderful characterization on screen and stage are funny and clever enough; now she's gone into print and the results are just as hilarious.

Our recipe for Zuckerman's Survival Cake is inspired by the story of her tortoise, which she supposes is a Jewish pet — "It knows its place. Outside on the lawn. It doesn't bark. It doesn't tear the Dralon. And it never raises the question of Kosher dogfood." (Unlike the Rosenthal cat — Pushkin — who is bent on interior undesigning in a big way.)

The story of Zuckerman, who refused to wake from hibernation and was eventually snatched from the jaws of death by a mouthful of apricot, is told in Maureen Lipman's book, *How was It For You?* (Published by Robsons Books). Read. Enjoy. You'll love it.

Here is a little taste:

"When I arrived home, it was to find Jack, Ruth and the kids and the corpse (?) of Zuckerman, standing contemplating the pantry. Jack had a small syringe in one hand and two cotton buds in the other, and was engaged in the mind-boggling decision of whether to give the patient warmed up chicken soup or tomato soup. For obvious reasons, that night Zucky ate Jewish.

...... Sweating with triumph at the amount accomplished so far, Jack gazed up through soup-misted glasses and said, 'I've got to get him some herring. It's full of iron.'

Each day, Zuckerman's smorgasbord grew more varied, until at last the day came when, confronted by iceberg lettuce and wild strawberries, he gave in; opened one eye, raised his upper jaw and clamped it firmly on the lettuce. He didn't eat it you understand, but it was a start".

★　★　★　★　★

Zuckerman's Survival Cake
(A baked Apricot Cheesecake)

4oz/125g dried apricots
6 Digestive biscuits
1oz/25g butter
1lb/450g cottage cheese
3 large eggs (separated)
4oz/100g caster sugar
1oz/25g cornflour
2 tablespoons soured cream
1/2 pt/10 fl.oz whipping cream
2 tablespoons apricot brandy
1 heaped tablespoon toasted almonds

- Put the apricots into a saucepan with enough water to cover generously. Bring to the boil and simmer for about 45 minutes or until the fruit is soft and the water almost gone. Allow to cool.
- Melt the butter. Crush the biscuits to fine crumbs and combine with the butter. Spread over the base of a buttered 8 inch spring-clip tin.
- Puree the apricots, add the cheese and sour cream, and blend or process well until the mixture is smooth. Beat the egg yolks with the sugar until pale and fluffy. Add the cornflour. Add to the cheese mixture. Whisk the egg whites until stiff, and fold into the cheese mixture, as evenly as possible without ever mauling it.
- Put into the tin, smooth the top and bake at gas 4 (350°F) for 1 hour. Turn off the oven leave the cake inside for a further 15 minutes.
- Whip the cream with the apricot brandy and fold in the toasted almonds. Serve generously with the cheese cake. If fresh apricots are in season, serve these in addition. If eating on a low table in the garden watch out for tortoises.

★ ★ ★ ★ ★

☆ ☆ ☆ David Bellamy ☆ ☆ ☆

The delightful professor has provided some interesting challenges, as you might imagine. He has two chinchillas, "Chillii" and "Con" – one likes chocolate digestive biscuits, and the other hates them. They also like eating drying-up cloths, and we hope that they will try the pudding cloth from the fig pudding, by way of a change!

"Pussyfoot", the Siamese, likes water on which Eichornia Crassipes (Water Hyacinth) and Azolla Filiculoides (Water Fern) float. He prefers this to fresh clean water. (We had a sheepdog who drank from the lavatory, given the chance; but then he also ate knickers on a fairly regular basis, so perhaps we'll leave him out of this).

We suggest a "paw bowl" for Pussyfoot, with his favourite flowers floating, with the same for guests' fingers after manhandling crevettes or prawns.

The Bellamys also have a swan, "Wellington", who likes to eat the floral pattern on the carpet! This sounds expensive, and a little inconvenient. Hopefully your cooking will at no time resemble the texture and taste of Axminster, but we suggest a way of preparing onions that may fool Wellington.

As many destitute owners will testify, animals are very fond of furnishings, and indeed furniture. We know of an otherwise delightful boxer, never left alone for long, who has eaten two three-piece suites and most of a Ford Sierra. Another acquaintance has had her driving seat reduced to a commode by her most refined little spaniels. There could be a market for vinyl or tweed-flavoured Bonios.

David Bellamy's passion for flora and fauna have taken him all over the world: it's impossible not to get involved when you see and hear his overwhelming enthusiasm. He has combined his love of nature and his gift for communication to work for conservation – to the advantage of us all.

★ ★ ★ ★ ★

Fig And Walnut Pudding

1lb/450g dried figs (chopped and stemmed)
2oz/55g chopped walnuts
6oz/170g flour
1 teaspoon nutmeg
12oz/350g suet
3 eggs
grated rind of 2 orange

14fl.oz/400ml milk
2 teaspoons baking powder
1 teaspoon cinnamon
8oz/225g granulated sugar
6oz/175g fresh brown breadcrumbs
a pinch of salt

- Bring the figs and milk to the boil and simmer gently for 20 minutes. Allow to cool. Sift the flour, baking powder, spices and salt into a large bowl.
- In a processor mix the suet and sugar, then the eggs. Stir in the bread and orange peel, in another large bowl, and gradually add the flour mixture and then the fig mixture, blending well each time. Pour into a 4 pint/2.25 litre pudding basin or mould, and steam for 2 hours.
- Serve with brandy or rum butter. This makes a delicious alternative to Christmas Pudding.

★ ★ ★ ★ ★

Onions Wellingtonia

This is not so much a recipe, more an exercise in trigonometry!

Per person:

1 large onion (red if you can find them)   salt and black pepper
1 tablespoon olive oil
2 teaspoons wine or herb vinegar

- Trim the root end of the onion, but leave intact. Stand onion on root. Cut parallel slices vertically at 1/4 inch intervals, but stop 1/2 an inch from the base. Swivel the onion 90 degrees and cut more vertical slices to form a crosshatch pattern, stopping 1/2 an inch from the base, as before. (Still with us?!)
- Soak onions in iced water for up to 4 hours, or until they have "flowered".
- Drain upsidedown on kitchen paper for 15 minutes.
- Put each onion on a piece of foil, base down, and pour over the oil and vinegar. Season with salt and pepper. Seal each onion in the foil and bake in a hot oven gas 8 (450°F) for about 30 minutes.

"Pawnote"

It would be very sad if all breeding were to be regimented with everything that moved being spayed, castrated or otherwise nipped in the bud, but there are definite drawbacks to owning a canine Lothario. Not that bitches are without blame – far from it! Twice a year our Jack Russell was putty in the paws of a neighbour's voluptuous Dachshund, who would sprawl temptingly on our garden path until she got what she thought she wanted.

What *we* got was the blame for owning a dog rapist, and a very stroppy neighbour with several litters of "Jackshunds".

If you are the desparate owner of a roaming Romeo or, like Diana Rigg, a "Fireside Lil", you may like to know about this "anaphrodisiac" we came across. We offer no cast-iron guarantees, so no paternity suits please if it doesn't work! Our vet confirms that in this dosage it's a harmless brew, and it is made from herbs known for their mild sedative qualities. Nevertheless, please do not exceed the dose or give to young or sick animals. (It is also recommended for humans, by the way, so be warned!)

If the "person" in question is in ghastly terminal stages of love-sickness, with doe-eyes, much sighing and moping about and complete anorexia, then it may be too late! If, however, he is in the devious earlier stages and still eating, try the following:

★ ★ ★ ★ ★

Pasta Caring

1/2oz White willow bark *(Salix alba)*
1/4oz White water lily *(Nymphoeaodorata)*
1/4oz Hops *(Humulus lupulus)*
1/4oz Comfrey root *(Symphytum officinale)*
1pt/20fl.oz water

- Crush the herbs in a pestle and mortar. Put into an enamel saucepan and add the water. Partially cover the pan and bring to boil. Simmer for about 20 minutes or until the liquid is reduced to half. Strain and allow to cool. (This will keep fresh for about four days in the fridge – please label it carefully!)

To serve:

We have found that pasta of all kinds is universally popular with both dogs and cats. Either cook some specially – any variety will do, and there are lots to choose from these days – or use left-overs from your own meal. Dogs don't mind a bit if it has congealed into a rubbery white cow-pat. Roughly chop up the pasta into bite-sized chunks and pour over two tablespoons of the "calm-down/stay-at-home" herbal mixture. Add a good portion of a favourite tit-bit – chicken, rabbit, cheese or anything that will ensure that the whole lot is eaten, but avoid red meat, garlic and onions.

The main idea of this meal is to encourage him to stay at home. Even if the herbs don't work, the food alone should slow him down!

(If you have difficulty obtaining the herbs, please write to us with a s.a.e. c/o the publisher.)

Our Publisher, Jane Tatam, relaxing with her cats.

Finale

Throughout this book we hope that we have been able to show what an important role pets play in many of our lives, and what fun and fulfillment they give. On a more serious note, we beg animal breeders not to breed indiscriminately.

A recent report from the R.S.P.C.A. revealed the shocking truth, that around 1,000 dogs are destroyed every day! On the other side of the coin, if you are thinking of purchasing a pet, especially at Christmas, please consider carefully the commitment you would be making, and the costs that would be involved; take into account the life expectancy of the animal, the food and vet's bills, and your own particular life-style.

If, for whatever reason, you have to deny yourself an animal, then all is not lost! You can still play a very worthwhile part in animal welfare by contributing in some way, however small, to an animal charity.

Here are a few suggestions, not in any special order.

R.S.P.C.A.
Causeway, Horsham, West Sussex RH12 1HG

International League For The Protection Of Horses
67a Camden High Street, London NW1 7JL

P.D.S.A.
PDSA House, South Street, Dorking, Surrey RH4 2LB

A.S.P.C.A.
441 East 42nd Street, New York 10128, USA

Howletts Zoo Park
Port Lympne, Lympne, Hythe, Kent CT21 4PD

The St Andrew Animal Fund
10 Queensferry Street, Edinburgh EH2 4PG

Lockwood Donkey Sanctuary
Wormley, Nr Godalming, Surrey

Cats Protection League
17 Kings Road, Horsham, West Sussex RH13 5PP

List of Recipes

Starters

Main Courses

Afters